Drama of Color

Drama of Color

IMPROVISATION WITH MULTIETHNIC FOLKLORE

Johnny Saldaña

HEINEMANN
Portsmouth, NH

Heinemann
A division of Reed Elsevier Inc.
361 Hanover Street
Portsmouth, NH 03801-3912
Offices and agents throughout the world

Acknowledgments for borrowed material begin on page 168.

Library of Congress Cataloging-in-Publication Data

Saldaña, Johnny.
    Drama of color : improvisation with multiethnic folklore
    / Johnny Saldaña.
        p.   cm.
    Includes bibliographical references.
    ISBN 0-435-08667-7
    1. Ethnic folklore—Study and teaching (Elementary)—United
    States. 2. Folk drama—Study and teaching (Elementary)—United
    States. 3. Multiculturalism—Study and teaching (Elementary)—
United States.   I. Title.
GR105.S33   1995
372.64'2—dc20   95-13203
                                                     CIP

Editor: Lisa A. Barnett
Production: Melissa L. Inglis
Cover design: Julie Hahn

Printed in the United States of America on acid-free paper
10 09 08 07 06 VP 10 11 12 13 14

To my parents
Isabel Martinez Saldaña and Dominga Olivo Saldaña
who gave me the best of multiple worlds

CONTENTS

ACKNOWLEDGMENTS

Many thanks are offered to the artists and teachers of *all* colors who shared their experiences or reviewed the chapter on working with children of color: Julie Benitez, Norman Brown, Linda G. Cook, Don Doyle, Mark J. Fraire, Lorenzo Garcia, John Huang, Sarah Hudelson, Daniel A. Kelin II, Mary J. Kelly, Coleen Koester, Lê Phạm Thúy-kim, John Lehon, Hiroko Matsumori, Virginia Pesqueira, Betsy Quinn, Tracy Joy Randolph, D. David Spencer, Mary Swierceski, Jesús Treviño, and Carlos J. Vallejo. Appreciation is also extended to selected writers of works in drama with children whose methods and philosophies are embedded in my own practice and in this book: Ruth Beall Heinig, Nellie McCaslin, Geraldine Brain Siks, and Winifred Ward.

My thanks and appreciation are extended to Stephanie Hettmansperger and Claudia Foster for allowing me to work with some of these stories in their classrooms; Elizabeth Harnett for pilot testing some of the session designs; Jeanne Belcheff and the Arizona Commission on the Arts for their professional support; the teachers, mentors, and colleagues who shaped my methods of doing drama with children: Dorothy V. Dodd, Coleman A. Jennings, Katherine Franklin, and Don Doyle; Lin Wright, the most influential person in my professional development; Lorenzo Garcia, for challenging and reawakening the Hispanic spirit within me; Lisa A. Barnett, Melissa L. Inglis, and Heinemann for their opportunity and nurturing; and Jim Simpson, for his time, support, and devotion in helping me realize this project.

Introduction

It's difficult to reach consensus these days. "Context," "ambiguity," "it depends," "multiple perspectives," "respect for diversity," and "let's agree to disagree" are just a few of the phrases you hear and read.

It's also difficult to reach consensus about terminology, particularly with labels for a cultural group (or should that be an ethnic group? racial group?). If I use the word "Anglo," which I hear broadcast on my local television news by people from that cultural/ethnic/racial group, some will take offense to the term and tell me they prefer to be called "Caucasian," "White," or "European American." I understand how they feel. If you call me "Chicano," "Latino," or "Mexican American," I don't take offense, but I do have a personal preference for what I label as my *ethnicity*: *Hispanic*. Those are my terms of choice. And we are a country privileged with choices and with the freedom to make them.

Attempts to define the terms *multicultural* and *multicultural education* are just as difficult. Each school system seems to have its own philosophical base and definition for the terms. (It's difficult to reach consensus these days.) Not only are culture, ethnicity, and race involved, but so are gender, social class, disability, sexual orientation, and other distinguishing characteristics that classify and categorize each one of us. Multiculturalism is, of course, becoming more prominent in education as the diversity of children increases in scope and number. Over two million school children currently enrolled have little or no knowledge of English (Gray 1993, 69). We read projections that by the year 2000 one in every three children in the classroom will be a child of color (ASU Center 1990, 1–3). By the year 2020, approximately half of all children enrolled in schools will be non-White (Banks 1994, 286). And by the year 2056, no ethnic/racial group is expected to be in the majority in the United States (Marvel and Kessler 1994, A6). As the cultural and ethnic compositions of our schools change, so do educational philosophies and approaches to teaching. I prefer not to define *multicultural education*, but instead, refer the reader to the masterful works of James A. Banks (1987; 1993; 1994) for direction and guidance. This book adopts Banks' view of a central purpose of multi-

ethnic education: the development of ethnic literacy in children. Ethnic literacy, to me, is knowledge about and respect for the traditions, history, values, languages, art forms, and literature of various ethnic groups in our world.

The study of an ethnic group's folklore is just one part of developing children's ethnic literacy. These canons of literature reveal much about the heritage, traditions, values, and symbols of an ethnic group, in addition to the common bonds that link us together as human beings. Ethnic foods, holidays and observances, and historic figures of color who have made important contributions to our country have their place as content in multiethnic education. My approach is not meant to exclude these topics, but to focus on the oral traditions from selected groups. Visiting the past allows us to see what differences emerged in each culture's genesis. Visiting the past is essential to examine and place our present condition into perspective.

The anthology in this book includes folklore from four broad ethnic and cultural groups: Hispanics; Native Americans; Asians and Pacific Islanders; and Africans and African Americans. But within the four groups, the stories are selected from a limited number of nations (for example, the Asian and Pacific Islands canon includes stories from Taiwan, Vietnam, China, Japan, and the Philippines, excluding material from Cambodia, Korea, Laos, the Hawaiian Islands, and many other cultures; the Hispanic canon includes stories only from Mexicans and Mexican Americans, excluding Cuban, Central American, Puerto Rican, and other related canons). Ironically, this attempt to be more inclusive with drama materials for children is also exclusive, since it omits so much and so many other cultures, such as Jewish American and European American. But it is a beginning. Each teacher is encouraged to extend her own knowledge about folklore, multicultural education, and children of color into the gaps I may have left.

My personal goal for drama with children is not to develop formal acting skills but to use the art form as a method to provide each participant with personal insight into the multiethnic world in which we live. Hence, this book is intended as a teacher resource for *enhancing children's ethnic literacy through drama*. Folklore from different ethnic groups can be used as a springboard for examining different ethnic perspectives and worldviews. And if stereotypes can be dispelled along the way, so much the better. I recoil when I introduce a Native American tale in a drama session and a child raises his hand and says, "How!"; when I discuss an Asian story and a child presses his hands against his head to slant his eyes; when I work with an African folktale and a youngster says, "Booga, booga." These responses, triggered perhaps by nothing more than playfulness, are rooted in misconceptions about people of color. I've encountered racism and discrimination from White adolescents and adults. But oddly enough, no child has ever made what I have interpreted as a racist remark when I work with Hispanic stories. I think they realize I'm "one of them" and they become more cautious (or conscious) of their behavior. That in itself may be noteworthy, but it doesn't stop me from educating them even more about my own or other ethnic groups.

Drama's terminology is also in flux. Book titles of related works will call the art form "creative drama," "theatre arts," "dramatic arts," or "improvisation." I chose the word *drama* for this book since *theatre* has connotations of performance, which is the opposite of the approach I advocate in this work. Multicultural education texts repeat frequently how their descriptions of selected cultural and ethnic behaviors are not universal but general traits found among particular groups. I cannot emphasize enough how this folklore-based approach to drama with multiethnic themes is just one of several available to teachers. Story drama, in which literature is used as the framework and springboard for dramatic activities such as pantomime and verbal improvisation, is a personal preference of mine, yet only one of several methodologies I use in actual practice. I also stay away from terms traditionally relegated to formal theatre production and use more process-oriented language with the elementary grade levels. In *drama* (not theatre), we *explore, practice, play out,* or *improvise* before we *share* our *work*—we never rehearse and perform a script. We don't have an audience in the classroom—we have *observers,* and we never critique—we *assess.* The Selected Bibliography of texts in drama will provide multiple perspectives on the art form, and teachers are encouraged to seek the methodology or methodologies which best suit themselves, their objectives, and their children.

Story drama with multiethnic folk literature integrates content in social studies, language arts, and drama. The study of a folktale and its related components (ethnic origin, motifs, characters, symbolic meanings, etc.) provides opportunities for both historic and contemporary interpretation of a culture's worldview. Within the content areas, specific objectives related to the dramatization may also be explored. The accompanying session designs after each story in the anthology draw from the following list of objectives (adapted from the Social Studies, Language Arts, Literature, and Dramatic Arts Essential Skills of the Arizona Department of Education 1989–1990):

SOCIAL STUDIES	DRAMA	LANGUAGE ARTS AND LITERATURE
• locate a country on a map or globe • describe how our world is multicultural and multiethnic • discuss similarities and differences between cultures	• portray a variety of characters • use dialogue to tell the story through improvisation • develop risk-taking skills for improvisation	• relate literature to personal experiences • compare/contrast literary works • participate in discussion • write original works (essays, etc.)
• develop personal and interpersonal skills through group collaboration • discuss how a story reflects the lifestyle of the people • discuss the connections between ideas and behaviors • recreate past history through enactment		
	• listen to and demonstrate comprehension of a story • identify elements of a story (setting, character, theme, etc.) • develop listening and oral language skills • select language appropriate to the context (e.g., character, historic period) • discuss universal themes in a story	
• develop critical thinking and problem solving skills • demonstrate persuasive and oratory skills by taking an issue and working towards reasoned solutions • develop multicultural perspectives through role taking • explore the human condition of past and present cultures through their history, geography, social climate, arts, and literature.		

School programs that are whole language based, or are exploring complex learning or integrated/interdisciplinary approaches to curricula, may find story drama compatible with their goals and an exciting, new approach to learning. The accompanying session designs are written for beginning teachers of drama and include a detailed outline of activities and suggested directions for student players. Integration of the three major content areas profiled above is a "given" in the session designs. Follow-up activities in social studies and language arts/literature are provided after each plan. Teachers can enhance learning in one or more subject areas with their own classrooms as they see fit.

The session designs are also in harmony with selected content and achievement standards for theatre from the *National Standards for Arts Education* (Consortium of National Arts Education Associations 1994):

Grades K–4: "The content of the drama will develop the students' abilities to express their understanding of their immediate world and broaden their knowledge of other cultures." Students:

1. "collaborate to select interrelated characters, environments, and situations for classroom dramatizations"

2. "improvise dialogue to tell stories, and formalize improvisations by writing or recording the dialogue"

3. "imagine and clearly describe characters, their relationships, and their environments"

4. "use variations of locomotor and nonlocomotor movement and vocal pitch, tempo, and tone for different characters"

5. "assume roles that exhibit concentration and contribute to the action of classroom dramatizations based on personal experience and heritage, imagination, literature, and history"

6. "collaboratively plan and prepare improvisations and demonstrate various ways of staging classroom dramatizations"

7. "explain how the wants and needs of characters are similar to and different from their own"

8. "analyze classroom dramatizations and, using appropriate terminology, constructively suggest alternative ideas for dramatizing roles, arranging environments, and developing situations along with means of improving the collaborative processes of planning, playing, responding, and evaluating"

9. "identify and compare similar characters and situations in stories and dramas and about various cultures, illustrate with classroom dramatizations, and discuss how theatre reflects life" (30–32).

Grades 5–8: "The drama should also introduce students to plays that reach beyond their communities to national, international, and historically representative themes." Students:

1. "individually and in groups, create characters, environments, and actions that create tension and suspense"

2. "analyze descriptions, dialogue, and actions to discover, articulate, and justify character motivation and invent character behaviors based on the observation of interactions, ethical choices, and emotional responses of people"

3. "in an ensemble, interact as the invented characters"

4. "lead small groups in planning visual and aural elements and in rehearsing improvised and scripted scenes, demonstrating social, group, and consensus skills"

5. "incorporate elements of dance, music, and visual arts to express ideas and emotions in improvised and scripted scenes"

6. "describe and compare universal characters and situations in dramas from and about various cultures and historical periods, illustrate in improvised and scripted scenes, and discuss how theatre reflects a culture" (46–48).

Generally, theatre is perceived by some Americans of color as elitist and reserved for the affluent mainstream. Financial and transportation resources may not be readily available to lower income families for live theatre attendance. But the opportunity for *all* children to explore the art form *in the schools* is readily available. These opportunities will be provided if administrative support for the arts is evident, and *if the individual classroom teacher integrates these experiences into her curriculum*. A teacher colleague shared that he finds classroom drama a financially accessible art form because the cost of producing it is minimal. "Sets and costumes cost money. But imagination and creativity—those are free, in ample supply, and donated willingly by my children."

Another friend of mine observed, "People are so easily offended these days." Interviews and discussions with teachers in preparation for this book generated heated debate from some on the role of drama with children of color, and multicultural education in general. No doubt there will be something in this book that offends someone, whether it be a particular story selected for the anthology, recommendations for working with children of color, a suggested activity or method for dramatizing the tale, a philosophical point of view, or even an omission. "Political correctness" is either an admirable goal or the stifling of free speech, depending on your perspective. Since it's difficult to reach consensus these days, let's agree to disagree. I ask you to extend allowances for my first major publication on multiethnic topics in drama. I feel honored to have this forum for expressing my ideas, but I encourage my readers to choose ultimately what works best for them. We are a country privileged with choices. This book is just one of many available to you.

1

Story Drama in the Classroom

This chapter is structured as a series of questions and responses. The questions are ones that have been asked most frequently by classroom teachers and college students on how a story drama is planned and conducted. The chapter is an overview of the most basic methods for story drama but is not intended as a definitive guide. Leaders who continuously dramatize material in their classrooms will eventually discover their own strategies and the methods that best suit them and their students. The bibliography of texts on drama with children also provides additional resources for you to read and integrate into your own practice.

The anthology of stories and the accompanying session designs in Chapters Three through Six are intended as frameworks for informally dramatizing folk literature. By no means are the recommendations the only way or even necessarily the best way to plan and conduct the sessions. They are simply documentation of the methods I have used in the classroom in my approaches to the stories and their dramatization. Teachers who select other pieces of folk literature can use these session designs as models for planning and conducting their own work with children.

Time and Space

How much time will it take to do a story drama with my class?

The average school day is a busy one. The daily schedule is usually regimented into specific time blocks for specific content. There is a lot of required material to be covered by a teacher and her students. How can "one more thing" be squeezed into the school day?

Teachers who value drama personally or believe the art form offers affective benefits for their children are more likely to make drama a separate subject during the school day. A typical session can last anywhere from thirty to forty-five minutes, depending on the way the teacher constructs and conducts the session. The grade level of the children (and their attention spans) should also be taken into consideration. A maximum of thirty minutes for kindergarten through first grade is suggested, of forty-five minutes for second through fourth grades, and of one hour for fifth and sixth grades. These maximum time blocks are arbitrary. Some primary grade children, if engaged with the material and the activities, can sustain interest for at least an hour. If your class schedule permits only thirty minutes for a story drama, then the session can be designed and led to fit the available time. Working under a time constraint sometimes makes the session more efficient by motivating you to select the true essence of the story to dramatize. But never feel compelled to rush through material for the sake of staying on schedule. A story drama can be explored over two or more separate sessions if student interest is sustained.

The Introduction noted how story drama with folklore can relate to social studies and language arts/literature. Time already scheduled for these subjects can include story drama as an alternative teaching strategy to explore academic material in a more participatory and experiential manner. Programs with separate time blocks for classes in multicultural education may find story drama a useful addition to the teaching repertory of classroom lecture, discussion, and audio/visual presentation.

When is the best time during the school day to do a story drama?

Teachers often have no choice in deciding when their classes go to lunch, the library, physical education, or school assemblies. They may meet concurrently with other classes for reading groups or "buddy" programs during specific time periods. Bad weather or half-day inservice programs may set an alternative schedule in motion. When does a drama session get scheduled? Realistically, whenever it can and whenever it's convenient.

But from my experience, the early morning hours are best for story drama because that is when children tend to be the least disorderly and most alert—qualities essential for the concentration demands of a story drama. If drama is to be integrated with a regularly scheduled subject area during the school day, conducting the session during that period makes common sense. A time block immediately after an afternoon recess also works well for some groups; the physical energies of children have had some release and their focus can be more easily redirected. Drama, or any art for that matter, should not be substituted for the student's recess period. A resentment is observed in children, and their motivation for effective work during a story drama is lessened.

Finally, if appropriate and as you feel comfortable, the "teachable moment" that occurs spontaneously during a class day is worth pursuing with a story drama. This moment occurs when the class's interest in a particular topic is so strong that it deserves tangential exploration. If the content of these stories or the lesson's objectives are relevant to a teachable moment, by all means pursue them.

How often should story dramas be conducted with my class?

This, too, depends on the amount of available time in your curriculum. The teacher pursuing growth in children's dramatic skills may observe little change if drama is conducted only once a week. Continued practice does, indeed, lead to enhanced nonverbal and verbal expression in drama. In the best of all possible worlds, drama every day should be the norm. In the real world, a minimum of two drama sessions per week is ideal.

A sense of continuity is established for children if sessions occur on regularly scheduled days and times, and the drama concepts and skills taught in the sessions are reinforced when distributed throughout the year. A story drama "unit" pursued over one week's time for the entire school year does little to develop children's skills in the art.

My classroom is small. How much space will I need for conducting a story drama?

A lack of adequate space for drama is one concern expressed most often by teachers. The number of movement experiences appropriate for thirty children in a standard classroom space with desks and chairs is obviously limited. But there are a few strategies that can be used.

In primary level classrooms, an open space in the corner of the room is sometimes available in addition to the desk or table area. Not only is this effective for storytelling, but it is also suitable for most story drama work. Depending on the physical activity needed in the story, children can work in the aisleways of their room. If possible—and it almost always is—desks, chairs, and tables may be pushed to the walls of the classroom to create a larger center space for working. Rather than a general call for everyone to "Push back the desks," have students do it a row at a time or a section at a time. Develop a routine for students to "prepare the room for drama."

Another alternative is to seek available spaces within the school. Sometimes an empty classroom with no furniture is available. By arrangement, the teacher can use an open area of the library, music room, media center, or all-purpose room when not in use. Though cafeterias, gymnasiums, and outdoor playgrounds are available, these spaces are too large, noisy, and distracting for young people trying to concentrate on the drama. A stage defeats the purpose of informal work, since the focus is on the process of creating, rather than on a finished product for performance. Young children may misunderstand the idea behind story drama if their working space is a theatre or auditorium.

There is a drawback to using a larger alternative space in the school. A different space may create more classroom management and control problems for the teacher. But if the same rules practiced in the classroom are observed and enforced in the alternate space, then children can keep some continuity of conduct.

Dramatizing a Story

How do I prepare for a story drama session?

The kind of preparation you undertake for a drama session depends on your objectives for the session. Is the purpose to enhance drama skills? to enhance ethnic literacy? to develop group skills such as interpersonal behaviors? When your particular objectives have been clarified, then other decisions can follow.

For example, if one of your objectives is to introduce your students to Hispanic culture in America, your research into the subject may include such topics as demographics, diversity of nationalities, and cultural differences from and similarities to the mainstream population. The folklore of the culture is just one of several areas for exploration, and dramatization of that literature is just one of several approaches to multicultural (and drama) education. As you read folklore from a particular culture or ethnic group for classroom use, find selections that appeal to you. This will increase your own motivation for preparing and leading its dramatization with your students.

You can choose to read the story aloud from a text (whether it be in a picture-book format or from an anthology of folk literature), but the most engaging practice is to share the material through the oral tradition. There are several excellent texts that address methods of storytelling (see the Selected Bibliography), and special considerations as they relate to story drama will be explained later.

If the story you've selected lends itself to dramatization—that is, if the action of the story can be interpreted physically or verbally, or both, and provides engaging activity—brainstorm ideas for how it might be dramatized with your children. The options and decisions fall into four major categories:

1. MOTIVATION: Find strategies to focus the children's attention on the content of the drama and to "mind-set" them with a particular mood, line of inquiry, etc.

2. PRESENTATION: Share the story with children. Read aloud or retell the selection with any changes necessary for its dramatization.

3. DRAMATIZATION: Facilitate the enactment of the story by the students. At times, you will play a role in the dramatization to enhance the playing by children. At other times you may be, for lack of a better term, "directing" the dramatization. There are many options available to the leader and her class for designing the session and the dramatization. More detailed methods will be described below.

4. ASSESSMENT: Provide time for reflection on the work, both from your point of view and from the students'. Since assessment obviously relates to the objectives, discuss the learning or experiences that took place. Reinforcement of or elaboration on the content can be conducted through follow-up social studies or language arts/ literature activities.

One of the most common problems for people new to story drama is giving children inadequate directions for their work. Practice aloud what you would ask or tell students so that they have specific tasks for more effective work. Image your class dramatizing the story in your classroom space. Also image things that could go wrong. If you're aware of particular children who may not be engaged with the drama, or of activities that could lead to misbehavior, then your directions can be re-examined to describe not only what you want the children to do, but also what they are *not* to do.

How do you begin the story drama? (Motivation)

"Today we're going to dramatize a story" may be an introductory phrase that's educationally sound but dramatically dull. A teacher colleague says she tries to "hook" children into the session from the very start. This implies that there are several ways to "bait" that hook.

Music from the story's country of origin is an excellent tool for establishing mood. Not only can the music be played at the beginning of the session, but also it can be played softly during the presentation and dramatization, if appropriate.

Visual Materials shown before the story focus a player's mind-set. Artifacts, crafts, and other objects from the particular culture under study arrest a child's visual attention. If these materials are not available, large illustrations or projected slides that relate to the content of the story can be shared. Visual stimuli are particularly helpful for young children and children who have difficulty with attention and participation.

Class Discussion on a topic related to or suggested by the story is also appropriate, particularly if social issues (poverty, the environment, sexism, etc.) are themes to be explored through the dramatization. Thought-provoking questions posed by the leader provide more student involvement with the material than a lecture.

Gaming provides active physical participation and involvement from children. A theme-related activity, such as the game of Opposites before "Little Eight John" (see Chapter Six), may generate excitement for the session and its content.

The session designs for each story will describe several strategies for motivating players' interest. Not all ideas have to be employed. Use only enough to capture the children's attention and interest, then proceed to the presentation of the story.

How do I tell the story to the children? (Presentation)

Books on storytelling will describe how to take personal ownership of a tale and to retell it with effective vocal and physical techniques. For purposes of this section, strategies and advice are limited to areas that relate to a story's dramatization.

Most teachers are more effective storytellers than they believe. Many already read aloud from picture books and novels for their classes. But when it comes to retelling a story in their own words without a written text, many are reluctant because

1. they feel it is easier to read the story from a written text;

2. they feel it would take too much time to commit the story to memory;

3. they feel inadequate as a storyteller.

Professional storytellers advise against memorizing written folktales word-for-word. If the material is presented by memory, the teller runs the risk of giving an artificial interpretation, since it is the writer's and not the teller's "voice" that is being heard. There is also a chance that the storyteller may forget a passage or important point, thus breaking the continuity essential for the presentation.

Though memorization of the entire story is discouraged, key words, phrases, or passages often can be committed to memory, especially at the beginning and ending of the story, for a smooth and exciting introduction and conclusion to the retelling.

If stories include dialect in written form (e.g., African American stories retold by Virginia Hamilton), the teacher is advised not to re-create the dialect unless she feels comfortable doing so. It may also be a matter of whether such attempts at dialect would be culturally sensitive to children of color in a classroom. Obviously, artificial attempts at an Hispanic dialect by a non-Hispanic for a Mexican American story might be embarrassing for children from the ethnic group. When in doubt, use your own natural voice for all narration and dialogue. If a story is written in a particular dialect, retell the tale in language comfortable for you.

Reading aloud from a book is a literacy behavior some teachers like to model for their children. If you feel more comfortable reading the stories aloud directly from this book, rather than retelling them in your own words, I encourage you to do so. Besides, the cultural integrity of selected stories will be maintained. There is value in hearing authentic tales collected "in the field" ("The Ram in the Chile Patch," "Why Bears Have Short Tails"); those retold by authors of color ("It's the Pichilingis Again," "People Who Could Fly"); or those stories whose primary source is a citizen of the country from which it came ("Auntie Tiger," "The First Monkeys"). Reading aloud with expression also serves as good preparatory work for storytelling without a text.

How is the story dramatized by the group? (Dramatization)

Just as the actor has two tools—a body and a voice—dramatization by the child can be done in two ways: nonverbally or verbally (or a combination of both). When you're planning specific methods of enactment for particular units of the story, consider whether the action suggested by the story is better dramatized through *pantomime* or *verbal improvisation* or both.

> *Pantomime:* This may include everything from a simple gesture (such as begging), to a character activity (such as eating vegetables in a garden or weaving a basket), to movement as a character (such as shaping one's body into a dog, a parrot, or a spider; moving across the space as a member of royalty). Pantomime is used in dramatization expressly for nonverbal communication of action. This method is most suitable for young children; older children become more physically and socially self-conscious, and pantomime activity in front of others as observers may be uncomfortable for them.

> *Verbal Improvisation:* The spontaneous generation of dialogue is done in role as a character and uses a scenario, rather than scripted lines from a written play. With young children (grades K–3), the leader can facilitate and oversee their nonverbal activities without participating in role. But if verbal improvisation is a key component of the dramatization, then leader participation, usually as a character, is essential. The leader can ask specific questions in role, thus generat-

ing more dialogue from children. Left on their own to improvise in a structured story drama, most young children may be at a loss for words ("I don't know what to say"). They may also feel the need to repeat any dialogue the way it was shared in the presentation of the story. Encourage them to develop their own dialogue as long as it is appropriate to the character and setting.

Children in grades 4–6 may also need the leader to participate in role when they first begin dramatization, but can be "weaned away" as they become more proficient at verbal improvisation. Their oral language skills and social development also permit more small-group work for verbal improvisation. Leaving them alone to plan their own scenarios and dialogue is a first step in developing independent work.

Most of the session designs accompanying the anthology include both nonverbal and verbal activities.

There are only a small number of characters in a story and I have a large number of children in my class. How do I get everyone involved?

Another way of phrasing this question is, "What are ways children may be grouped to portray the characters in the story?"

Ensemble: Ensemble is a term used in this book to describe all children playing the *same character* at the *same time*. For example, a story may have one main character at the beginning or middle involved in some type of key action (such as Anansi trying to free himself from a sticky trap in "Anansi and the Sticky Man," or rodents gossiping about a cat in "A Holy Cat"). Some stories may ask all children to play the same role through most of the dramatization, such as Bear in "Why Bears Have Short Tails." Each child, whether at a desk or in a designated part of the room, is doing the same activity under the leader's guidance. This casting structure is most appropriate for young children because it provides maximum participation and interest; it allows all children an opportunity to experience a character's development or primary action; and it explores all available roles within a story before choosing a particular character for the rest of the dramatization.

Pair Playing: Each child works with a partner in a private, separate space. Each pair works simultaneously on some unit of action from the story. This structure is obviously appropriate for portions of a story that feature two characters interacting with each other. For example, one child may be playing the little girl Chuan while a partner takes on the role of Auntie Tiger (see "Auntie Tiger"). The two improvise a dialogue in which the Auntie tries to convince Chuan to let her inside the house. Each pair within the class improvises simultaneously, but for the sake of time and interest, each pair's work is not usually presented in front of others.

Split-Half: Half of the class plays one character simultaneously while the other half takes on a different role simultaneously. This differs from pair playing because one half serves as observers while the teacher works with the other half in the dramatization. For example, in "The Medicine Man," girls are asked to play Thought Woman while the boys take on the role of Coyote. Roles are reversed after the first playing of the story. Split-half playing does not always have to be according to gender; it may simply be by numbers when there are two primary characters or groups of people in the story. In "Taro and the Magic Fish," half the class portrays sea creatures while the other half portrays an army. These two groups also participate simultaneously after observing each other's work.

Small Groups of Three to Five: Children are grouped with no more than five participants to work on a particular unit of action within the story. For example, in a class of thirty children, there may be six groups of five children. Each group may be asked to practice a particular portion of the story to dramatize. Each group's work is then presented in the order that their units occur within the story (see session designs for "The Weeping Woman" and "Little Eight John"). But there may be other stories that are dramatized in which each group works on an idea based on the story, rather than on linear events that occur in the story itself (see "It's the Pichilingis Again" and "Auntie Tiger"). Since several independent decisions have to be made in small groups, and social skills are needed for group work to be effective, this structure is better reserved for fourth grade and up. Third graders with some drama experience in ensemble, pair playing, and split-half playing may be able to work effectively in small groups.

Individual Roles: Each child has a specific role to play in the dramatization of the story. This casting structure is usually reserved for stories with a large number of characters, for older groups, and for groups with a substantial amount of drama experience. There is a significant amount of preparatory planning and organization required for the distribution of roles among the class. None of the session designs in this anthology utilize individual roles, although "The Weeping Woman" is perhaps the most complex in terms of casting.

Solo Work: One child (or a small group of children) has a specific character to portray in front of other children serving as observers. In "The Poor Widow Bullfighter," a small group of children is asked to improvise scenes with the principal characters while other children observe and comment on the work. This type of "spotlighting" should be reserved for upper grade levels, or for classes with some experience in drama and risk taking.

These are just six options for organizing children and distributing the roles. The number of characters in a story or a unit of action may indicate which method is more appropriate. And since characters enter and exit the action of the story, more than one casting method can be employed within a session design. The children's grade level and their amount of drama experience may also be considerations that determine which casting structures are used. Ensemble, pair playing, and split-half playing are the easiest. Small groups of three to five, individual roles, and solo work are more difficult for younger or inexperienced children and make more facilitation demands on the leader.

How do I decide which child plays a particular role?

Depending on the way the distribution of roles is designed, children may *volunteer* to play a particular role; they may be *assigned* a particular role by the leader; or within a small group, they may *distribute* the roles among themselves.

When volunteers are selected to play particular roles, the leader can identify which children have an interest for certain roles. But not all those who volunteer may be proficient at playing. There is also disappointment expressed by the young if a certain child did not get selected for a role. Those who do not volunteer may be the ones who could benefit from playing a particular character. As children are given more experience with story drama, some may begin anticipating which role they would like to portray as the story is told by the leader. Children may make their preferences overtly known to the leader as soon as the story is over (sometimes *during* the storytelling). The enthusiasm is refreshing but scattered, and the teacher should make certain that the distribution of roles is handled in an orderly manner. After being "mobbed" by children immediately after I finished telling a story, I began saying, "I'm going to choose people who are sitting quietly with their hands raised for the roles." They accommodated me quickly.

When the leader assigns a child a particular role, it is done as an offer rather than an order. The child should be given the option to turn down a role; asking a child to play a particular character in whom there is no interest may be detrimental to the dramatization. The leader can offer the role to a child who is excited about the character, thereby ensuring a more effective playing; or to a child whom the teacher feels can benefit from playing a particular role. Rather than a blanket assignment such as, "Linda, you be the general from the opposing army," you might rephrase the invitation: "Linda, I'd like to see how you portray the general from the opposing army when you confront Taro by the seashore. Are you willing to try that role?"

When children are placed in small groups of three to five, the leader may elect to have children within the group distribute the roles among themselves. This is certainly an opportunity for group decision making and consensus. But some conflicts could arise within a group over "who plays what" if the group is not mature enough or has not had sufficient experience in group process skills. Anticipate the problems that may arise, and collectively discuss how a group can go about distributing the roles equitably, democratically, and agreeably. The session design for "It's the Pichilingis Again" is geared specifically for this objective.

What role do I as the leader play in a story drama session?

The leader is always a facilitator of the session. She guides children through the process of creating a story drama by organizing the decisions made both before and during the playing. The basic tasks are no different than the teacher's functions during any other subject taught in the classroom: manage the session, present new information, guide the activities, lead a discussion, ask questions, etc. The session designs accompanying each story offer both detailed descriptions for conducting the session and recommended questions and directions for players, scripted as a model to consider and adapt.

Sidecoaching, a term that refers to the leader offering verbal prompting or directions to students as they dramatize, is a method of further guiding and enhancing children's work. For example, sidecoaching may mean offering directives as children pantomime a particular activity, as in "Fatima and the Snake": "Pick up a long stick and show that you're digging the earth for yams. Now try to show through your face and body that it's a very hot day, and you'd rather be playing in the shade than working in the sun."

Sidecoaching may also include suggestions, verbal encouragement, and assessment as children are working: ". . . and you'd rather be playing in the shade than working in the sun." "Wiping your forehead is a good way to show that you're hot. What other things can you do to cool down?" "Excellent—now that's a different way to show you're trying to cool down."

Leader or *Teacher in role,* or portraying a character from the story in the dramatization, is important when the story calls for facilitation of the session as an active player with children. Playing a role is particularly encouraged when working with young children or novices to drama; when student involvement tends to be hesitant; and when verbal improvisation is a critical component of the dramatization. Teachers in role assume selected characters not because children won't be able to portray them, but because children will become more actively engaged with the playing when they assume their own characters interacting with the leader's. Children new to story drama (or, as later profiled, selected grade levels and cultural groups) may feel awkward and uncertain with dramatic tasks if left on their own to create characters and dialogue. But when the leader as a character from the story asks questions in role and facilitates verbal improvisation, the children are provided assistance with expressing language. With young children it is particularly important for the leader to state when she is and is not in role: "I'm going to play the Fox now," or "I'm not playing the Fox anymore, I'm me."

Teachers new to drama are no different than some children in one regard: portraying a character is sometimes perceived as difficult to accomplish. I do not believe that teacher hesitancy is due to a reluctance to participate, or a fear of appearing "foolish" or "childish" in front of their students. Though teachers are not always able to articulate the real reasons for their own anxiety, their discomfort may be rooted in a mistaken assumption: "I can't act." I reply to that, "It doesn't matter. Because in a story drama you aren't 'acting' anyway. You're *playing,* or you're *working,* or you're *improvising,* or you're *assuming a role in an informal classroom drama,* which is much different than performing on a stage—which you aren't doing."

If you read aloud to your children from picture books or novels, you might have "played a role" when you gave a character's dialogue a little more "feeling" when you became personally involved with the material. Teachers also adopt a personality in front of their classes that is much different from the personalities they display with adult peers and family members. Technically, you're playing a role each day in your classroom and you're improvising every day with your students. I've heard it reported in teacher training workshops that a teacher makes approximately 200 decisions of one kind or another each *hour* in the classroom. Some of these decisions are language choices for lecture, discussion, conversation, and other oral tasks. The flexibility essential for classroom instruction develops the ability to change and adapt at a moment's notice. The ability to "think on your feet" is essential to improvisation—and a skill already possessed by most teachers.

Do we dramatize the story all at once or one part at a time?

For most stories it is helpful to divide the material into sections or *units*. Playing the entire story nonstop without adequate preparation and planning invites disaster. By dramatizing one or more units at a time, the players will be able to focus their creative energies on a story segment with more detail. A *unit playing* can be determined using the following guidelines: a major change in time or setting, the introduction of new characters, or a new sequence of action. In the session design for "The Medicine Man," each unit of the story is dramatized for more detailed development of characters and dialogue. Character work is first done with children portraying Thought Woman, followed by children portraying Coyote. The next unit brings the two characters together for a small exchange of dialogue. This is then followed by dramatizing Coyote's journey, then another exchange of dialogue between Thought Woman and Coyote. A new character, Mouse, is introduced, thus starting another unit of action. Bringing Mouse and Coyote together for the final unit of playing completes the dramatization. Assessment of the players' work after each unit also assists with the process of character development and deeper reflection on the material.

A *complete playing* is dramatizing the story "from beginning to end without any stops." But this approach is recommended only after the story has been explored through unit playing first. Once children have practiced and embellished each unit, the entire story can be dramatized with minor prompting from the leader. Teachers are encouraged to "walk children through" the action before putting all the units together.

Replaying a dramatization is another option if interest is sustained; if a different way of dramatizing the action is explored; if assessment determines that children may benefit from another playing by improving work in a particular area; or if children are rotated to play different roles. Available time is the determining factor in whether a replaying is conducted or not. But if student motivation is high, replaying a story drama is encouraged—as long as children continue to commit to the action and concentrate on their work.

There are some exceptions to the above. The session designs for "The Warning," "The Ten Farmers," and "A Holy Cat" are termed *holistic*. Children are thrust into the dramatization of the stories' primary action without presenting the story first. It is a method of allowing the action to unfold and taking the story in directions determined by the children. The stories are used as springboards for exploration of their themes, rather than dramatization of their story lines. The session designs will provide more detail on the holistic structure of dramatization.

How is the work shared in the classroom?

Depending on the casting methods chosen and the particular dramatization structure, work can be shared in one of three ways:

> *Unobserved with full participation* means that all children are working simultaneously in ensemble, pair playing, or individual roles. There is no "audience" because all children are playing a role and involved with the dramatization in some way.
>
> *Observed in an ordered sequence* usually refers to small-group playing. In "The Weeping Woman," for example, the entire class is divided into small groups, with each group developing a particular unit of the story. Each group then shares their work in front of the others in the order the units appear in the story, logically providing a "beginning, middle, and end" to the dramatization.
>
> *Observed in a random selection* generally refers to small-group work. In "Auntie Tiger" and "It's the Pichilingis Again," each group is asked to develop and dramatize an original adventure featuring characters from the tale. But the order in which each group shares is not critical since there is no linear format they must follow. Each group's work stands independently from the others.

What do I look for in the children's work? (Assessment)

Assessment, of course, depends on the objectives established from the beginning. Each teacher may have her own particular agenda for student achievement in such areas as drama concepts and skills (e.g., oral fluency in verbal improvisation, sustaining a character, recall of story line); personal and interpersonal behaviors (e.g., concentration on the task, volunteering for a role, cooperation in a group); or related concepts and skills in social studies or language arts/literature (e.g., ethnic literacy, recognition of theme, identification of protagonist and antagonist). Whatever the focus or purpose of the story drama, assessment—which includes student reflection—is an essential part of the whole. One teacher found no purpose for documenting children's progress in drama in written form: "If it's not for a grade, why bother?" Assessment does not necessarily mean that checklists must be used to tally points for a cumulative letter grade for children's work in drama. But, as another teacher put it, reflection on the work will "cement the knowledge" gained through the experience. The following strategies are some recommendations for assessment.

The teacher as assessment instrument for drama provides personal perspectives to children on their work. After the session, personal observations are offered on what the leader saw and heard—both effective work and work that could be developed in the future. Rather than assess a child's playing with an overall "Good," point out specifics that made the child's work effective, such as "When you played Anansi you shaped your body in a very unique way to create a spider," or "Your dialogue flowed very well. I didn't hear any hesitation in your voice—you were very confident with what your character needed to say." Continual verbal and nonverbal praise go a long way in motivating student work in drama. Preparatory encouragement before an activity begins, sidecoaching during the playing with positive reinforcement, and assessment of effective work after the dramatization frame the session with a supportive atmosphere.

Children should also be given the opportunity for self-assessment. Asking what players enjoyed the most about the session is a simple diagnostic for gathering positive experiences. But children's self-assessment can go further. Asking what players enjoyed or found effective about other players' work begins the aesthetic response process. Once players have an understanding of the challenges posed by dramatization, they may also begin to examine which portions of the story were difficult to enact, or which characters were difficult to portray—and why.

Asking players to reflect on alternative choices for the dramatization is another exercise in enhancing critical thinking skills. Such questions might be, "If we were to replay this story again, what might we do differently to make our work even more effective?" "When we dramatized this part of the story, we had a problem [specify: overlapping dialogue, loss of concentration, etc.]. What could we do to solve the problem if we replay the drama?" "What part of the story was most important and how can that be emphasized through another dramatization?"

A student reflective journal for drama may provide children with the opportunity not only to exercise writing skills but also to privately voice their experiences as players. Among practitioners, the perceived value of a written journal as an assessment instrument for drama is mixed, but some teachers advocate its usefulness as a means of individual student assessment—a procedure difficult to pursue during whole class work.

Art work done by young children after the session may extend the creative and artistic side of drama even further. Projects or content related to the cultural origin of the stories are most appropriate. One practitioner teaches fundamentals of costume design to her children, and post-session artwork focuses on the possible clothing and accessories that might be worn by selected characters if the story were to be formally mounted as a theatre production. She also finds art projects an effective means of reflection after drama since some of her non-English-speaking children cannot participate fully in discussion or write adequately in the language for a journal entry.

Videotaping sessions for viewing by the children and for leader review may be helpful if the objectives relate to the development of drama skills.

Videotape may also be useful for the teacher to assess her own facilitation of the drama, to have a more permanent record of children's work, or to research some component of classroom drama. Some classes find that the video camera distracts and inhibits participation. Others find it a common piece of equipment in our multimedia age and take no notice of it. Some cultures or religions may object to videotaping, and in some schools parental permission may be needed to use this media tool.

Whether assessment in drama is rooted in state curricula or national standards, teachers should examine if objectives, expectancies, etc., may be Eurocentric or incompatible with the learning styles and everyday realities of children of color, particularly children from lower socioeconomic backgrounds (see Chapter Two). Standards for assessment exist as admirable goals for drama programs, but if teachers maintain other agendas for their work, such as enhancing ethnic literacy, then assessment should focus on the related objectives.

Management

I've tried drama in my classroom but the children get disruptive. What are some ways to control and manage the session?

Physical/Spatial Methods: Some teachers are reluctant to rearrange the desks, chairs, and tables in their classrooms to provide adequate space for drama. Keeping the environment intact helps establish a sense of continuity for them. Depending on the activity, some dramatization activities can be played easily with the desks and chairs in their regular places. Children working while seated, standing next to their desks, or playing in the aisleways are other possibilities. In some primary-level classrooms, an open area is provided for storytelling and other whole class activities; this, too, provides a moderate amount of space for story drama.

Eventually, teachers and children can develop a routine for rearranging the desks, chairs, and tables to provide as much space as possible for more physical activities. As long as children can be seated on the floor in a circle or in an oval with adequate space between them, there is enough room for dramatizing a story.

Establish boundaries where children can and cannot work: "As you move around the space as Coyote, stay away from under the desks and tables and work in the center area only." It is also worth spending time teaching children how to "find your own space" and "work in your own space—a part of the room where you can stand in the middle or at the sides so that no one will be disturbing you." This will be utilized primarily for ensemble playing.

Also spend time teaching children how to move in slow motion. References to the television and film effect, or modeling by the teacher, will help children grasp the idea. If the teacher feels a planned activity has the potential for becoming too frenetic in "real time," asking children to dramatize nonverbal activities in slow motion may prevent some problems from occurring.

If the teacher observes one or two individuals not focusing on the work she can use the standard techniques of establishing eye contact with the children, walking toward them for proximity, and touching them gently to monitor and acknowledge their inappropriate behavior. If energies become too scattered, there is nothing wrong with stopping the session to ask children to join hands in a circle. All then drop their hands and sit collectively to discuss the problem.

Areas with too much space, such as a multipurpose room, gymnasium, or a stage should be avoided. Unless the teacher and students have developed an effective working relationship where respect for boundaries is followed, larger spaces may not be as effective as the children's own classroom environment.

Oral/Aural Methods: A leader's vocal tone and volume level are perhaps the most effective means for influencing group dynamics. Some of the best teachers (and classroom managers) of children I have observed speak in a gentle but confident, medium-paced, moderately soft voice. If motivation or energy in the group is needed, an enthusiastic voice can initiate the work. If the energies are too scattered, the leader's reduction of her own vocal volume and rate can quiet the group. (These are, of course, ideal guidelines. Depending on the group and the teacher, the opposite might hold true.)

Developing a repertory of verbal signals helps the leader with directions and control. Using such words or phrases as "Freeze," "Relax," or "Start bringing your work to a close" after a group activity helps children bring closure to open-ended work. Children can be taught to listen afterward for the leader's next set of directions. There is also more control established when the teacher uses what may be seemingly obvious words for starting children on their work: "Go" or "Begin." These provide an impetus for purposeful activity. Surprisingly, many beginning leaders don't use these simple words to initiate the children's playing after a series of directions.

Sidecoaching can weave control measures with directions. For example, if children are transforming from human beings to monkeys in "The First Monkeys," and a burst of strange noises from children is anticipated, the leader might sidecoach, "Start changing your body, without any sounds, from a human into a monkey; silently, silently, your body changes shape, and you're too scared to speak or make a sound."

Musical instruments such as small drums and tambourines work for some leaders, but they seem to lose their effectiveness with a group after prolonged use. The novelty of instruments with unique sounds, such as an afuche or a vibra-slap, are more useful as sound effects rather than control devices for enhancing a dramatization.

Tape-recorded music can be used as a signal for children to start and end their work. If the music is related to the culture under study, or enhances the mood of the playing (somber, comical, etc.), so much the better.

Visual Methods: Hand signals that indicate the group is to begin, end, or become quiet for further instructions may work effectively if the group is fairly focused and responsive to the leader. With more verbal groups, however, hand signals may be useless if children's energies become scattered and visual attention is not given to the teacher.

Flicking the room lights can work as a control signal. But like musical instruments as control measures, they may not be immediately accessible when needed. Dimming the lights in the room, when appropriate to the session, creates a different environment and motivates through novelty.

Continually sweeping the playing space with your eyes and sending messages nonverbally with your face are perhaps the best visual control measures readily available.

It's difficult to get my children committed to the drama. How can I get them to concentrate on their work?

I discovered at one session that I took too much for granted. I was wondering why one child was having so much difficulty focusing on the work after I repeatedly asked her to concentrate. The answer became obvious when she asked me, "What does *concentrate* mean?" Some teachers ask their children to "focus" or to get "on task" when they need them to concentrate. I use the phrase, "Think about this and nothing else" as an initial way to get children to understand the concept and affective behavior of concentrating.

Another seemingly obvious answer is to provide *specific* directions for the activity or objective. Beginning leaders may take too much for granted when they ask children to "Be a mouse" or "Be sad." Those seemingly simple directions are fraught with problems. In one approach to formal actor training, the actor is taught that one cannot "be" something or "be" in an emotional state. Instead, the actor is trained to *do*. Instead of saying, "Be a mouse," a more direct *doing* activity might be, "Shape your body as if it were a mouse and explore ways you might move across the space looking for plants and herbs." Instead of "being sad," ask the child to do things that accompany sadness: "Show how your face and body might look after your pet parrot has flown away, and walk back to your seat without any fake crying. Really try to focus on how the character might feel. Go."

Several of the techniques discussed in this chapter can enhance concentration in the players. Providing visual stimuli related to the session, such as unique cultural artifacts, can motivate children's interest in the content. Asking children to close their eyes during some activities can shut out distractions, but not all children readily volunteer to close their eyes. Asking children to work in their own space is another technique for enhancing concentration, but is limited primarily to ensemble playing. Sidecoaching from the leader can enhance the playing by verbally prompting, motivating, supporting, and encouraging children as they participate.

Throughout this book the words *play* and *work* are used interchangeably. But each word has different connotations for children, and word choice may also have an impact on resulting concentration. "Let's play out this story" creates a different frame for the dramatization than "Let's work on this story." The leader's tone and attitude toward the drama may be readily perceived by children. If drama is approached frivolously or as "a good substitute for recess in winter" (Ritch 1983), then children will not take the work seriously. But if the teacher's tone and attitude reflect a sense of value and purpose for the activity, then children may be more committed to the tasks.

Despite various techniques and methods for getting children to concentrate, the bottom line is to ensure that the material is *meaningful* and *relevant*. When meaning and relevance are high, then motivation to work is generated and concentration in the work is enhanced. In other words, help children see the payoff.

What are some common problems with verbal work?

No matter what grade level, children will be at various levels of comfort when it comes to verbally improvising in front of others. Among certain children for whom English is not their first language, comprehension and oral response may be inhibited if the session is conducted exclusively in English. Yet some studies in drama suggest that second language skills can be developed through improvisational activities (see Chapter Two).

Some of the most frequent problems encountered in verbal improvisation stem from:

1. the shy or inhibited child, whose participation is minimal or nonexistent. Leaders can encourage their participation through the use of narrow questions that solicit "yes," "no," or other one-word responses leading to more complex answers through broad, open-ended questioning techniques. Forcing the child to respond, or waiting an uncomfortable length of time for the child to respond, may be detrimental to future participation. But for children in bilingual, ESL (English as a Second Language), or LEP (Limited English Proficiency) programs, the pause a leader gives and the patience she demonstrates after her question may be essential for ensuring participation.

2. awkward group improvisation. When small groups are asked to develop an improvisation there may be only a few who initiate dialogue and carry the scene. In some groups there may be an erratic flow to the dialogue and hesitancy or uncertainty from some of its members. This may not necessarily be indicative of children incapable of improvisation. It may be more indicative of a weak or vague improvisation scenario they were asked to develop.

3. unconventional or inappropriate responses. The child who goes for a "quick laugh" from others with a facetious response contributes to a disruptive atmosphere. Leaders have several options, depending on what they feel is most appropriate at the time: a quick, stern glance; stopping the session to discuss the student's believability and commitment; or encouraging the student to rephrase the response in a more appropriate manner.

Some children may respond with an anachronism during a session. In a dramatization of "How Mosquitoes Came to Be," a Native American origin story, one fourth-grade boy slew the giant saying, "I'm gonna cut you up like a pepperoni pizza!" Stopping the session to point out the anachronism was just one of the 200 decisions per hour I considered at the time. But since the response did not break the commitment from other children, I let it pass. During the assessment that followed, however, I asked players about the appropriateness of that response. The young boy's line was generated from excitement with the action, not from facetiousness. Historic setting was forgotten for the moment (and was a difficult concept for him to grasp in the first place). We discussed how pepperoni pizza would not have been a part of the historic Tlingit culture, and how anachronisms might inadvertently enter verbal improvisation with folklore.

What are some common problems in small-group work?

Take time to discuss how to work effectively in a small group. Let children know what problems may occur before they actually begin, and what solutions are available to them should they encounter one of those problems. The session design for "It's the Pichilingis Again" is an exercise in orienting children to small-group participation, skills, and dynamics.

If a small group appears to have difficulty generating an idea or reaching consensus, the leader can hear what ideas have been generated thus far and offer suggestions for directions or choices. Rather than mandate or select the best idea, the leader can suggest to the group, "It sounds as if that last idea is the most playable in the time you have to work, and offers everyone a chance to take on a role. Consider that one as you make your final choice." Only if the group has developed no ideas for playing should the leader offer a specific idea for their improvisation.

When one group states, "We're ready," while other groups need more time to practice their work, the leader can ask that group to practice their work again: "An improvisation changes each time it's done. Go through your scene again to make sure everyone is participating and knows what everyone else is doing." If the teacher can spend time with the group, she may ask them to share their work for her so she can offer feedback and suggestions for clarifying the ideas presented in the scene.

The one group that may not be finished with their work when the others are ready to share should not be made to feel inadequate, nor should the rest of the class be made to wait while they continue working. If the group states, "We're not ready," the leader can reassure the entire class with, "I know you've only had a short time to develop these scenes, but let's see what you've created so far. Remember, this is not a performance, this is an improvisation." If the group feels reluctant to begin, the leader can either ask them to simply tell the class what they had planned to share if more time had been available to practice; or provide time during the session to work with the group while the rest of the class observes and offers feedback.

Conclusion

Profiled in this chapter are methods for informally dramatizing literature in the elementary classroom. The session designs after each story in the anthology (Chapters Three through Six) will illustrate specific examples of how a narrative text is transformed into a story drama. These designs assume there is a mainstream or acculturated population of children in each classroom. The next chapter discusses factors for leaders to consider in the preparation and playing of a drama session should children of color be present in the group—whether they are few in number or the predominant membership of the classroom culture. If you feel proficient working with young people from various ethnic backgrounds, proceed directly to the anthology. If you are new to multicultural/multiethnic education, you may wish to peruse "Drama with the Child of Color."

2

Drama with the Child of Color

Value the child as an individual and the culture as a whole.
                                                        Mary J. Kelly

Multicultural and multiethnic education texts often profile general characteristics of children of color. Teachers may use these profiles to better understand these children and to change mainstream curriculum, instruction, and assessment strategies to accommodate the needs of diverse classroom populations. Child-rearing practices and socialization among certain ethnic family systems will bring children of color with culturally-specific behavior patterns into the classroom. But to describe the "typical" Native American child is no easy task, for there are hundreds of recognized tribes and nations in the United States, all sharing some commonalities, but many with their own distinctive language, spiritual beliefs, traditions, and other cultural components. Ms. Kelly's introductory quote is a reminder that not all children from one ethnic or cultural group will behave exactly the same way. Multicultural education researchers emphasize this same cautionary approach. Generalizations from "recipe lists" of ethnic behaviors could lead to stereotypical teacher beliefs. Drama instructor John Lehon and selected colleagues from the New Orleans public schools feel that lower socioeconomic status makes more of an impact in the classroom and on the child's worldview. Multiple perspectives aside, there will always be individual children of color who demonstrate exceptions to generalized ethnic or cultural patterns of behavior.

Research Studies in Drama

Gourgey, Bosseau, and Delgado (1985) conducted a study with lower socioeconomic Black and Hispanic students in grades 4–6. Students partic-

23

ipated in an improvisational drama program over a six-month period. Gains were observed from students in vocabulary and reading comprehension. Improvement in attitude areas such as trust, self-acceptance, acceptance of others, and empowerment was also suggested by survey results.

An intensive six-week sociodrama program with African American kindergartners increased their oral language fluency (Haley 1978). Hendrickson and Gallegos (1972) observed significant improvement in English language proficiency from Mexican American children in grades 2 and 6 after a ten-week drama program. Vitz's eight-week program (1984) with a small sample of ESL (English as a Second Language) Southeast Asian immigrant children in grades 1–3 showed significant increases in the group's total verbal output.

Shacker, Juliebö, and Parker (1993) combined both second-language acquisition (French immersion) and social studies instruction through drama. The third graders improved their oral language skills and vocabulary in French through experience with different language functions in improvisation, plus they found exploring social studies through drama an immensely positive experience. In an informal report, Erdman (1991), an instructor of Spanish to elementary school students, observed that memorization of dialogue for short but formal play productions assisted in grades 4–5 with student recall of Spanish dialogue months later. An improvisationally developed piece with first graders using story drama techniques enabled them to recall their brief lines in Spanish up to a year later.

Gimmestad and De Chiara (1982) observed that play reading with scripts featuring ethnic characters and their struggles; combined with follow-up discussion, dramatization of scenes in small groups (with assured success), and other related curricular activities; enhanced children's knowledge about the ethnic groups under study. The project also served as a method of prejudice reduction among children in grades 4–6, primarily Puerto Rican.

Other research studies with mainstream, or mixed, samples of children suggest that drama may produce positive effects in such areas as self-confidence, empathy, and cooperation; assist with word and story comprehension among kindergartners (reported in Wagner 1988); develop self-esteem and moral reasoning (Kardash and Wright 1987); improve the social skills and self-concepts of emotionally disturbed youth (Buege 1993); develop reading readiness and increase literacy behaviors (Tucker 1971); enhance story comprehension through dramatization (reported in Wagner 1988); and, of course, improve dramatic expression (Kardash and Wright 1987; Rosenberg 1989).

The selected sampling of studies profiled above may attest to drama's potential for enhancing language and social skills in children. Research in multicultural education has resulted in general profiles of the learning and social behaviors of children of color. These observations may have implications for the way children of color participate in story drama.

The Child of Color and Story Drama

An ethnic minority child's level of acculturation into mainstream society may be an indicator of whether or not the child achieves competency standards from a mainstream curriculum. But failure to achieve those standards should not always be seen as failure on the part of the child. It is the curriculum itself and the teacher's approach to it that may have to be reexamined to be more compatible with the child of color. If traditional Eurocentric curricula and approaches to teaching are incompatible with the child of color's cultural background and conditioning, then academic failure is fostered (Burstein and Cabello 1989, 9). Educational equality is a primary goal of multicultural education, and its achievement requires changes in curriculum, teacher beliefs, teaching styles, and other personal and institutional changes (Banks 1994, 3–4).

Knowledge of the different cultural backgrounds (and hence, the needs and learning styles) of each child in the classroom is essential, particularly if a diversity of ethnic and cultural groups is represented. Coleen Koester, a veteran elementary classroom teacher, encourages her children to "feel free to tell me what they know," and takes time to find out why children act the way they do instead of judging the way they behave: "Is it cultural, or is it personal?" Daniel A. Kelin II, a drama instructor of Pacific Island youth, and John Lehon, of the New Orleans public schools, make learning reciprocal by asking children of color to assist them with appropriate choices for dramatizing their own cultural stories.

White and Hispanic drama specialists who work with Hispanic youth advocate that knowledge of and sensitivity to the children's cultural background, and acceptance of the Hispanic child's culture, are essential teacher characteristics. Listening and sensitivity are strategies they employ to achieve those characteristics, and flexibility with their planning and teaching is always present to adjust to the emotional and social needs of children. (This general advice is promoted by multicultural education specialists for other children of color as well.) Permitting the use of Spanish in addition to English for verbal improvisation, however, is determined by each teacher. One leader encourages the use of Spanish to make drama an "unconditional" experience for her lower socioeconomic youth in California. Other leaders report that their middle-class Hispanic adolescents prefer not to speak Spanish or have little knowledge of the language. The use of Spanish depends on the geographical and socioeconomic area in which they are working, the age of the children, specific school mandates or programs, and knowledge of the language by the leader and students themselves.

Teachers, therefore, should be cautious of broad statements and profiles about ethnic and cultural characteristics. Inferential leaps may be made incorrectly, and individual differences will be inherent within each group and setting. Following is a discussion of how selected ethnic and cultural behaviors *may* affect the way children of color respond to drama. Some are drawn from interviews or correspondence with practitioners; others are deductions based on multicultural and cross-cultural research; and some are based on my own experience. They are to be interpreted as *general guidelines*, not rules, when children of color participate in drama.[1]

Trust and Risk Taking

Building trust in the classroom is an essential component of any teacher's job and not reserved exclusively for drama. But since the art form asks children to share work in front of others, to be expressive nonverbally and verbally, and to take creative risks through spontaneity, the security to do this is needed by children first.

Some cultures may have norms of social behavior that could affect initial work in story dramatization. For example, there is a general hesitancy among Hispanic youth to make themselves "stand out." Depending on the mixture of individuals in the class, activities that set the self apart from the group are avoided. An Hispanic theatre artist shared, "We're taught to keep to ourselves—don't make a spectacle of yourself." The Native American child integrated into a mainstream school with a predominantly White staff may become isolated, shy, and withdrawn due to cultural dissimilarities between self and the institution (Baruth and Manning 1992, 45). Some Asian and Pacific Island cultures teach that attention drawn to oneself is improper. Teacher and parent Lê Phạm Thúy-kim shares that Vietnamese children are taught to listen more than to speak, and to withhold personal opinions from teachers. Drama specialist Hiroko Matsumori feels that asking the Asian Pacific immigrant child to exhibit selected drama behaviors too quickly may cause feelings of anxiety. Hispanic and African American children from lower socioeconomic levels may be taught by their parents or older siblings to be leery of White authority figures, including teachers (although positive school climates can counteract these beliefs). With these inhibitors to personal expression and trust in place, the risk-taking essential for drama may be difficult to nurture. Voluntary participation may be minimal; discomfort and hesitancy will inhibit expression in front of peers.

1.   For ease of reading, many citations have been deleted when appropriate. See References for a complete list of sources used for this chapter.

Norman Brown, a Dine (pronounced dih-NEH; Navajo) drama teacher, shares that establishing trust with his children is essential to begin the expressive work needed for his program. He gains this trust not only in the classroom, but also through members of the child's kinships and clanships. If a cultural group is predominant in the geographic area where one teaches, and the teacher is not a member of that group, Brown and Kelin suggest enlisting the advisement or services of a representative from that culture. This sends a message that respect for the people is held. Lehon, as a White male, makes a conscious effort to dispel any African American children's prejudicial attitudes toward his ethnicity and gender (i.e., authority figure) by taking himself out of the power role, when appropriate, and playing *with* children in drama. He also shares personal stories from his own background to help students feel more comfortable sharing their stories, and to help them find commonalities between the teacher and themselves.

Leaders may wish to introduce story drama "safely" by structuring nonverbal and non-threatening tasks in ensemble or simultaneous pair playing. Participation in the drama should also be optional rather than required. Some of the session designs in this collection are geared for beginning work ("The Ram in the Chile Patch," "Why Bears Have Short Tails," "The First Monkeys," "Fatima and the Snake"). Although teacher modeling of a dramatic activity is generally discouraged, demonstration for or simultaneous participation with the child may be useful when introducing drama in the classroom. Sidecoaching with positive reinforcement may also break down inhibitions during play. Teachers playing in role with children model the idea that assuming a character is acceptable. Soliciting dialogue through closed- and open-ended questioning will help players generate verbal responses, but care must be taken when using this approach (see "Verbal Improvisation" below). Assessment after the session might focus on the players' responses to the story and its dramatization, rather than teacher observations of drama behaviors and recommendations for more effective work.

Trust is prerequisite to risk taking. A supportive and encouraging teacher tone is perhaps the most effective method of establishing a secure environment for creative work to begin and flourish. Kelin and Lehon feel that a teacher who exhibits accurate and specific knowledge about a culture's history and literature sends an affirming, positive message to children from that culture. When children perceive acceptance and support, trust is earned.

Cognitive Styles

The majority of session designs outlined after each story in the anthology are linear, meaning that the stories are dramatized in a step-by-step, building-block manner. This is intended primarily as an aid for the beginning classroom teacher who may be unfamiliar with specific methods and techniques for organizing a story drama. But among African American children there is a preference to focus on the whole rather than the parts (Bennett 1986, 20; Kelly 1994). The linear designs of the sessions may also be incompatible with the holistic thinking of Native American youth and, according to some studies, Hispanic youth. Compartmentalizing a story drama may not be in harmony with their cognitive approaches to material, so more exploratory and open-ended structures for the drama may be preferred.

Bilingual educators Sarah Hudelson and Carlos J. Vallejo share that bilingual children tend to be more cognitively flexible and creative than monolingual youth. In a safe environment, these children are more readily able to deal with the ambiguous and unstructured. But for those still learning the language used primarily in the school, the cognitive demands of code-switching (see "Verbal Improvisation" below) can lead to frustration (Shade and New 1993, 320). For teacher orientation to the mechanics of story drama, linear structures may be best to start with. After experience with the art form, confidence will lead to more flexibility and spontaneity with the material (see session designs for "The Warning," "Auntie Tiger," and "A Holy Cat"). Paradoxically, there is the need for all students to have consistency and predictability while knowing that the teacher is also flexible. Finally, preferences for linearity and structure increase the higher one scales the socioeconomic ladder—across all ethnic groups.

Pantomime

The child of color's proficiency at or ability to pantomime and express ideas nonverbally through gesture, movement, or facial expression may not be influenced by cultural or ethnic background. Research and practitioner opinion are mixed on whether the African American child is more proficient at nonverbal communication and more expressive physically. Some multicultural education studies document these observations made by researchers, yet others of African American descent consider these characteristics stereotypes. It also may be incorrect to assume that dance, an integral part of many Native American cultures, provides a foundation for the Indian child's ability to move with ease in dramatic activity. Dance is part of the social and spiritual worlds of Native American culture, and whatever experiences the Native American child has had with dance may not transfer to the classroom drama session—not on the basis of proficiency, but from cultural taboo. In Dine culture, the physical portrayal of certain animal characters during a story drama, particularly with costuming, may be interpreted as sacrilegious by some since the act is considered the embodiment of the animal's spirit, not just a character portrayal. There may also be reluctance to portray selected animal characters, such as snakes and owls, due to their spiritual associations in a culture's belief systems. Kelin observes that certain movement patterns, reflective of Pacific Island culture, some-times work their way into the children's pantomime. He does not discour-age it but learns from it.

Eye Contact

Some cultures, such as Dine and Vietnamese, condition children to avoid eye contact with adults as a sign of respect. If this behavior transfers into dramatization work it should not necessarily be interpreted as a sign of passivity. Active listening and involvement may be present, and requiring the child to make eye contact during dialogue exchanges with the adult leader may send culturally conflicting messages to the player.

Emotional Expression

Brown, Lê, and Matsumori affirm that emotional expression among some Asian and Native American cultures is generally restrained or controlled as a sign of maturity. Similarly, among Hispanics such expression may be restrained from self-consciousness or adherence to a subgroup ethic, such as gang membership. Drama leaders seeking "proficient" portrayal of a character's emotions from children may not see expected results. Since a character's emotions in a dramatization may not be fully realized, teachers should not force them from children or assess their work as inadequate. Leaders can assess the child's cognitive understanding of a character's emotions through discussion. Expression *can* be obtained by the teacher's acknowledgement of what the student is being asked to do and how it may be "different" for them. Vallejo encourages teachers to ask children of color for their permission to explore emotional expression in drama, rather than to assume automatic compliance.

Gender and Cultural Dynamics in Small-Group Work

In story drama, pairs and small groups are formed sometimes by allowing children to select their own partners and group members. Group dynamics in a drama session may also be influenced by selected ethnic and cultural behaviors. In Asian Pacific and Hispanic American cultures, gender roles generally appear to be more rigidly defined within the family, with specific rules of conduct for and between boys and girls. These roles may influence the quality of individual drama work as well as small-group work when children of different genders are mixed together, particularly in the upper elementary grade levels. Girls may acquiesce to or be more reserved around boys in a small group. Allowing children to select their own small-group composition, which usually results in same-gender membership, may allow them to feel more comfortable working with each other. Once classroom trust has been established, and gender equity has been fostered in the classroom, a small group composed of both genders is worth exploring.

Hispanic, African American, and some Asian cultures show a preference for working cooperatively in the group setting (Chan 1983, 165; Bennett 1986, 303). Native American children tend to focus on community effort rather than individual achievement. Depending on the cultural and ethnic composition of the school and individual classroom, children of color may prefer friends from the same ethnic background (Baruth and Manning 1992, 65). But in classrooms where social climates are accepting, more interethnic friendships are found (Bennett 1986, 134). Since groups of children must work cooperatively for a specific goal in the session, encouraging or facilitating a mixture of cultural and ethnic backgrounds within each group may help children become more familiar with one another and obtain more positive attitudes toward one another (Banks 1994, 244). Classroom drama is a collaborative art and depends on group participation to succeed. The opportunities drama provides for developing group dynamics suggest that the art form can be a vehicle for enhancing interethnic relations.

Casting

Leaders who provide "educational equality" by allowing all children the opportunity to portray central characters, regardless of gender or ethnic background, will be adhering to a primary goal of multicultural education. Utilizing stories with females in prominent roles (e.g., "The Weeping Woman," "Auntie Tiger," "Fatima and the Snake") will also lend inclusion to the session.

In formal theatre production, "nontraditional" or "color-blind" casting is a strategy in current practice by many companies. Roles for a play are not necessarily cast according to the character's ethnicity or gender, but according to the sole criterion of the best actor for the role (unless, of course, the play specifies that a character belongs to a particular ethnic group and should be cast accordingly). In story drama, this same principle might be followed, depending on the cultural and ethnic composition of children in each classroom. If one Hispanic child is in the class, should she and she alone be given the opportunity to portray the role of Mariposa in "The Poor Widow Bullfighter"? Not necessarily. If that child volunteers for the role and appears eager to portray her, she could certainly be cast as Mariposa. But if "educational equality" and "ethnic literacy" are goals for a school program, shouldn't any non-Hispanic in the class, including a boy, be eligible for the role and possibly gain a new perspective by portraying it? Most certainly. Couldn't that Hispanic girl gain confidence in her ability as a player if she portrays the role effectively? Perhaps. But what if her cultural upbringing inhibits her from being so overt in front of a group? Then casting her in the role may do more harm than good. But what if the teacher feels that her portrayal of this role may enhance her self-esteem and develop more effective oral language skills? Then cast her.

It's difficult to prescribe any formulas or guidelines for this area. There are multiple factors to consider, as outlined above (It depends). Drama specialist Betsy Quinn notes that upper elementary students need preparatory explanations from the teacher about the purposes of and policies for "nontraditional" casting in classroom drama. Group acceptance of a student's voluntary choice to portray any character is encouraged, especially when a boy wishes to play a female role, or when White students volunteer to portray such characters as African American slaves. Teachers are encouraged to use their own discretion and judgment when casting children of any color for specific characters from an ethnic story.

Verbal Improvisation

The quantity and quality of verbal improvisation with children of color may be affected initially by their cultural backgrounds and proficiency with oral language. Trust between student and teacher is essential for any risk taking. And for verbal improvisation to be effective, the individual's willingness to risk must first be developed. But there are other cultural subtleties at work.

Verbal improvisation may be influenced by the Native American child's speech and communication patterns—delayed responses to auditory messages, speaking at a softer and slower rate, and less interjection during conversation (Baruth and Manning 1992, 41–44; Brown 1994). Lê and Matsumori share that some Asian and Pacific Island cultures socialize children to listen more than speak, and to speak in a softer voice. Selected Indochinese children may have difficulty with the pronunciation of English, adding more self-consciousness to oral expression. Teachers may wish to play in role more often to actively solicit dialogue responses from children. These responses may not be readily volunteered, and direct questioning strategies in role may be useful. But by no means should a response be forced from the child, and patience ("wait time") should be displayed during verbal interaction.

Foreman (1991) suggests that direct questioning for immediate response may be incompatible with the cultural learning styles of the Canadian Cree and Blackfoot. Questions should be posed for consideration and reflection first; responses will follow later. Once trust and student confidence are enhanced, oral language for drama may flow more easily.

Jordan et al. (1983) summarize studies with Hawaiian children's speech patterns in classrooms. One-on-one verbal exchanges between a teacher and an individual child do not necessarily generate desired responses. There is a preference for children to respond collectively to teacher questioning. Teachers accustomed to posing questions to or improvising with an individual child may wish to address the class as a whole. Individuals within the group may respond simultaneously, and the teacher can then respond to or acknowledge what is either consensus or one response heard among the individuals. Collective response from the group may also be a preferred classroom pattern of interaction with the teacher among African American youth (Bennett 1986, 23).

Some recent studies suggest that the African American child is socialized to be verbally expressive and demonstrative. "We have a culture that is of the oral tradition," says storyteller Mary J. Kelly. She and Quinn support the idea that dialogue for verbal improvisation should flow well from African American children, but not necessarily in a smooth "give-and-take" pattern of exchange. Interjections, primarily supportive and affirmative, are observed in everyday conversation (Baruth and Manning 1992, 65; 72) and may transfer into verbal work. Kelly allows the overlapping dialogue patterns, but spends time encouraging children to "listen"— an essential skill for improvisation.

Depending on geographical region and socioeconomic status, dialects, if any, may be difficult to understand by non-African Americans. Attempts to correct the speech (asking for clarity in articulation, proper tempo, etc.) may be essential for adult performers in formal stage productions, but not essential for process-oriented drama in the classroom. Prominent African American educators, however, recommend that teachers help Black children distinguish between what is proper speech and grammar at school and what is acceptable at home or in the community (Comer and Poussaint 1992, 211–12; 225–26; Hill 1989, 13). Kelly and Tracy Joy Randolph, two African American drama practitioners, disagree and feel that the use of Black English should be accepted unconditionally in any setting. If the goal of multicultural education is to help children become aware of other cultures, the use of Black English may be anachronistic if the African American child is improvising a Native American story set in a particular geographical region and time period (e.g., "The Warning" in Chapter Four). But if that African American child is new to drama, demands for "appropriate" speech and language may be inhibitors to initial participation. Quinn accepts whatever speech children bring into her drama classroom. Once trust has been established, she guides them in making choices that will help make their characters believable. Teachers are advised to use their own discretion and judgment on these issues. (It's difficult to reach consensus these days.)

Limited English proficiency will, of course, affect the child's verbal work in drama if English language instruction is predominant in the classroom. School programs realize the necessity of teaching English—the language of "access and success" in America (Finer 1990). But teachers must also value the child's native language to enhance the non-English-speaking child's self-esteem and self-concept, prerequisites to effective learning (Gonzalez 1990; Martinez and Dukes 1987). Kelin pauses deliberately at selected moments when he tells a story from the Pacific Island students' culture. They spontaneously verbalize what happens next and he incorporates their phrasing or native language vocabulary as he continues the tale to provide a sense of contribution and ownership for the group. Quinn allows "unconditional" language use in her drama classes and shares that there is a fascination from native English speakers for the native languages of ESL children.

As noted earlier, selected studies suggest that English or second-language acquisition may be enhanced through improvisational drama programs. Content that is relevant and meaningful to the child's cultural world, such as folklore, motivates engagement with the material. Though his work was with secondary school grade levels, Sanchez (1994) used international folktales in English with his ESL drama classes as translation exercises and as a springboard for examining cross-cultural similarities. Allowing children to use their native language or to code-switch (changing from one language to another throughout oral speech in bilinguals) may make initial sessions an unconditional experience for young people still learning the English language.

Assessment

Many Hispanics operate under the cultural concept of *dignidad*, and the child may be highly sensitive to praise and criticism. An Hispanic theatre artist shared that her culture is full of pride, but "that pride is easily damaged." Brown asserts that Native Americans have undergone generations of shame and oppression that still haunt them today, and the greatest harm that can be done to any people is to stifle their creativity. Asian Pacific Americans are sometimes stereotyped as the "model minority," reinforcing the false belief that they will automatically excel at school with little teacher intervention needed. For the older African American child, racism and oppression—from their most blatant to their most subtle forms—hinder positive development of self-concept (Baruth and Manning 1992, 81). Drama is not advocated as a panacea for all social ills, but it *is* promoted as one way of providing positive experiences for children of color and enabling them to see themselves in a more positive light. These experiences and perceptions, however, will depend not only on how the teacher conducts the drama but also on how she assesses it.

Reflection on and assessment of the story drama is primarily oral and facilitated by the leader through discussion and questioning immediately afterward. But teacher observations of children at work *during* the drama play a major role in the content of that discussion. Developers of alternative models of assessment encourage teachers to take children's ethnicity and language background into account when evaluating their work (Herman et al. 1992, 107). Koester uses assessment with her diverse classroom population both to reflect on the drama and to adjust her own teaching:

> Because you have kids that come from different places and ways, when you're teaching they're not going to conform to your expectations and the conflicts are always going to come up. But it's *how* you handle those conflicts or those ways. If you have a group of children not participating, then it's 'Why aren't they?' Not that they can't or won't . . . they're responding maybe to another influence. And that's a chance for *your* learning, is to investigate why. And I guess that's the broad picture of how I see diversity. If we come in with one strong teaching style and it's not working, then we need to change the way we teach. . . . We need to redefine what drama is and what we want from it and how it connects to the people that we work with and know.

Since assessment is tied to teacher objectives, specific guidelines are difficult to prescribe. Regardless of intended outcomes, teachers and fellow students should affirm the child of color's accomplishments in drama not only (or necessarily) in terms of a curriculum standard, but also in terms of what the individual has accomplished, how the individual has contributed to the group collaboration, and how the individual has grown in her ethnic literacy. Assessing interethnic relationships, based on interpersonal behaviors, is perhaps the one given in all drama assessment. Verbal and nonverbal praise are paramount for all children, but especially for those whose lives may be burdened by negative messages and treatment from dysfunctional families, lower socioeconomic conditions, and society in general.

Respecting the Literature

Just as teachers of drama need to be aware of how a child's cultural conditioning may affect drama behaviors, so should they be aware of how a cultural group's canon of stories and legends may affect content choices and approaches to the dramatization.

Hispanic

In some Hispanic folklore, religious content is prominent, particularly Catholicism. Characters that might appear are priests, angels, the devil, and historic religious figures. If the school administration and community are comfortable with religious themes or content being explored in class, then selected tales may lend themselves to story drama. Supernatural motifs and folk beliefs are also included in some tales (skeletons that fly, *La llorona*, folk medicine, etc.). Certain schools set policies restricting content that has overtones of satanic worship and other forms of the supernatural. But consider that mainstream western folk literature also includes supernatural elements (elves, witches, magic spells, transformations, etc.). Teachers should ensure that double standards do not exist for multiple canons of folk literature.

There are a few stories that include excessive violence (e.g., drunkenness, gruesome murder, etc.). This, unfortunately, is not only fiction; it is also part of our world today. Stories with this content provide immediate perception of truth in older children. Not all stories have happy endings or poetic justice (see "The Weeping Woman"). Death, cruel treatment, and anti-heroes can be found in several tales. But these stories can also be some of the most exciting and playable ones. It is the teacher who must ultimately determine their appropriateness for her class.

Teachers are also advised to be aware of stereotypes that appear in some adaptations or "watered-down" versions of authentic folklore sometimes seen in children's picture books. Not all young Mexican boys are named Pablo, and there is more to Hispanic culture than just fiestas.

Native American

Stories and legends told within Native American culture are not viewed as fiction. Active learning and the dissemination of cultural knowledge occur during storytelling. Elements of spirituality are also woven into many of the tales. If the leader approaches the Native American story as fantasy, the sanctity of the stories is negated for the Indian child. Depending on the specific tribe or nation, portraying selected gods or animals in a dramatization may be taboo since it is perceived as embodiment of that god's or animal's spirit. Teachers should check if such concerns might be held by the child's particular tribe or family before planning and playing the dramatization.

There is sometimes a mystique for non-Indians about the use of Native American materials. The proper use of stories may vary from nation to nation. A Dine tour guide in Arizona was explicit about the seasons when stories should and should not be told (winter and summer, respectively). He also shared that there are some stories unknown to outsiders told exclusively within the nation. When I asked a Cherokee storyteller in Tennessee about my use of the tales for story drama, he did not find offense in anything I was doing with them, nor did he prescribe any protocol for me to follow.

A White drama specialist shared that her non-Indian teacher colleagues are sometimes leery of using Native American stories and music for fear of using the materials inappropriately and offending their Native American students. As an example, I once unknowingly used religious ceremonial music during a powwow drama session, when a student noted I should have used music targeted specifically for powwows. I attributed my mistake to ignorance and learned something new about the use of traditional Native American music. Trial and error is one way to learn new information. But it is better to move forward in the light of knowledge than to grope in the darkness of ignorance.

If you are using materials from Native American culture, recognize that each tribe and nation has its own distinctive set of cultural norms and patterns. The "generic" Indian does not exist. Explore what makes the Hopi, the Choctaw, the Cherokee, the Pueblo, the Yakima, and other tribes distinctively unique. There are multicultures within this particular ethnic group.

Asia and the Pacific Islands

There are twenty-nine distinct subgroups of Asian Pacific Americans (Baruth and Manning 1992, 92). Limiting native folklore selections to the Japanese and Chinese canons excludes the Vietnamese, Cambodians, Koreans, Pacific Islanders, etc. It is difficult to profile such a vast body of folklore from so many countries. For example, in Japanese folklore appropriate for children, interactions between humans and animals are prominent, and cultural values influence character action and story structure (reported in Aoki 1992, 119; Matsumori 1994). Lê says that Vietnamese stories, fables, and folk poetry—some pieces thousands of years old—are still shared today in the oral tradition. There are some sophisticated themes, life lessons, and cultural knowledge contained in Vietnam's body of prose and poetry, a canon that loses some of its delight in translation. The Philippines have been influenced strongly by centuries of Spanish colonization. Some folktales from this country exhibit a unique blend of European and Asian motifs. "The First Monkeys" (Chapter Five) deals with an animal prominent in the country, yet also features a spiritual character reminiscent of Hispanic Catholicism.

Teachers searching for material from the Asian and Pacific Island cultures may find more authentic tales in collections compiled by anthropologists and folklorists, rather than picture books intended as children's literature. Contemporary fiction by such writers as Lawrence Yep provides dynamic and relevant material for Chinese Americans. Contemporary literature for children also explores the "newcomer" role of Asian Pacific immigrant children, and several titles profile the problems some may encounter at school.

African and African American

It is important to distinguish between the canons of African and African American folklore. They are distinctively different in content and tone, and both should be explored in the story drama experience.

African folk tales adapted for children's literature tend to focus on selections featuring animal characters. Although this provides playable material for story drama and wonderful possibilities for movement, stories with humans and animals interacting are also available in the canon. Males are prominent in the folklore, and storyteller Mary J. Kelly feels that the authentic tales are filled with symbolic sexuality and excessive violence (see "Fatima and the Snake").

Kelly also shares that African American folk tales seem to have transformed the violence found in African folklore into trickery and cleverness, representing the spirit of an oppressed people wanting to rise above their circumstances. There is ironic humor and pathos in some of the stories, and tales of slavery provide some of the most dynamic and playable material for story drama.

Early documentation of African American folklore was conducted primarily by White folklorists, and collections of these stories and anecdotes are written in language considered stereotyped and racist by today's standards. Renowned African American storyteller Augusta Baker shared at one of her concerts, "We have never said we were 'gwine t' do' *anything*." Interpretations and retellings of poignant and humorous stories from this canon by such African American writers as Virginia Hamilton and Julius Lester blend a contemporary flavor into their versions with careful attention to dialect and rhythmic language. These adaptations are perhaps more suitable for today's children.

The focus on African American literature should not rest exclusively on tales of slavery and oppression. Kelly shares, "It's important that we learn to exchange those positive things about our cultures." The study and use of stories, particularly *by* African American children, are encouraged to stimulate more reading and enhance cultural knowledge (Comer and Poussaint 1992, 278–79).

Finally, there is some content in tales that transcends issues of culture and becomes an issue of good taste and appropriateness for young children. Selected stories from any culture contain obscenity, sexual humor, or references to bodily functions (see "The Ram in the Chile Patch" and "Auntie Tiger"). Such stories are collected by anthropologists in the field and are valued as authentic. But if the story is worth dramatizing, teachers may edit the questionable passage from their retelling. Purists may object vehemently to this suggestion on the grounds of censorship or violating cultural integrity. But to me, the sensibilities of children come first. This is not to advocate censorship but to deal with the reality of what cannot (and should not) be discussed with young children in the classroom. If you're offended by what's on television, switch to another channel. If you're offended by one story, look for another. We are a country privileged with choices. The ultimate decision rests with the teacher and the community standards. It's difficult to reach consensus these days.

Finding the Universals

Our *differences* make us unique; they are what give us individual identity. Exploring the unique elements in these stories enhances cultural and ethnic literacy and may enable children to see things from others' points of view. The session design for "Taro and the Magic Fish" introduces children to the *mie* from the Japanese Kabuki theatre. "The Warning" attempts to make players reflect on the crisis faced by the Laguna Pueblo Indians when the Spanish explorers arrived on the continent. "The Weeping Woman" (*La llorona*), the most well-known folktale to southwest Mexican Americans, is surprisingly unknown to many non-Hispanics. A discussion of why the story is so popular among the culture reveals much about the ethos of Hispanics.

But finding the differences is just one component of multicultural education. Koester works with a broad ethnic mix in her classroom, and observes that each child begins the school year with an individual cultural background. Through conscious efforts by the teacher, the diversity eventually evolves into a unified "classroom culture." She notes that "we can't possibly share all of the cultural distinctions of the people that we teach. We all come from a place, and we're meeting people coming from other places, and somehow the goal is to come together and find our bonds." Differences are still acknowledged and celebrated as unique, but the universals—connections that link us together as human beings—are purposefully sought. Similarity of color or gender isn't necessarily an indicator of commonality. And sharing the same classroom space for several hours a day isn't necessarily an indicator of unity.

Helping children find the universals may also help them find personal *relevance* and *meaning* in the stories—reference points that link the literature of the past with the contemporary self. "The Ram in the Chile Patch" is more than just a simple formula tale of a ram who takes over a boy's chile patch by force. It is a tale of bullies who confront us in the school yard. It is a tale of gangs who take over our turf. It is a tale of how the little can overcome the big with simple and strategic ingenuity. "Auntie Tiger" and "Fatima and the Snake" remind us that there is danger in disguise—not just for adults, but for children as well; and not just in the fictional past, but in the present reality when we meet a stranger.

Through universals we can also help children make *connections* from one thing to another—reference points that connect the self with others. "It's the Pichilingis Again" includes mischievous characters that might loosely be labeled "Mexican leprechauns." Why do so many cultures have trickster characters in their literature? The story of "Why Bears Have Short Tails" is found not only among the Dine, but also among the Cherokee and in the folklore of Norway. How did this same story come to exist in these diverse cultures? What was the route of transmission? What are the connections? These are the questions whose answers provide our "common bonds."

Finally, each character in every story has *emotions*, advocated by drama practitioners as the most basic universal of all. Through literature and art forms, students can experience and reflect on the universal human condition through the emotions the characters undergo, possibly enhancing empathy for them (Bennett 1986, 197–98). If a child has experienced despair, anxiety, belittlement, humiliation, anger, confidence, triumph, or happiness, then she may find personal relevance and meaning in the character of Mariposa in "The Poor Widow Bullfighter." If a child wishes to be brave, powerful, and in control, then relevance and meaning may be found in portraying a soldier or sea creature from "Taro and the Magic Fish." And if the child finds joy and mischievous delight in trickery, then a connection is made with a Pichilingi, a Fox, Chuan, or Anansi in the stories that follow.

Conclusion

Again, not all children from one ethnic or cultural group will behave exactly the same way. There will always be individuals who demonstrate exceptions to generalized ethnic or cultural patterns of behavior. Hudelson, Koester, and other teachers observe that complex combinations of social variables affect children of color because they deal with multiple cultural worlds. But Vallejo advocates that when we are all reduced to the lowest

common denominator, "people are people." Establish a secure environment where children feel free to take creative risks and are motivated to
learn both the differences and similarities between their own culture and
another's. Help children discover what makes each one of us unique, then
find the universals to establish "common bonds."

The anthology of twenty stories and their accompanying session
designs are offered to teachers as one method of developing ethnic literacy
in children through the art of story drama. Since each classroom has its
own distinct culture and needs, feel free to adapt these lessons to meet
your children's needs and your own objectives. Kelly advises, "Be willing
to throw away everything you've learned and reinvent the wheel." But
above all, value the child as an individual and the culture as a whole.

3

Stories from the Mexican and Mexican American Canons

"THE RAM IN THE CHILE PATCH"

This tale includes the classic motif of the little triumphing over the big, and has a wide grade-level appeal: K–4. Teachers should feel free to risk assuming character voices for the Ram, Cow, Dog, Cock (change to Rooster), Burro (change to Donkey), and Ant during the storytelling. When some of the verbal exchanges between the characters are repeated, they could be deleted in the retelling. The dramatization works most effectively when the teacher plays the role of the Ram.

The story from Paredes' collection is reprinted with its original ending—wickedly delightful for some adults but inappropriate for young children. The solution to this problem is very simple and is described in the accompanying session design.

This was a little boy who had a little patch of chile peppers. He tended it with the greatest care. That was what gave him his livelihood. And then one day a little ram got into it.

So the boy began, "Little ram, little ram, get out of that chile patch."

"You unmannerly boy, what are you about? Get out of here or I'll kick you out."

41

"Little ram, little ram, get out of that chile patch."

"You unmannerly boy, what are you about? Get out of here or I'll kick you out."

Finally he did try to get the little ram out, and the little ram, instead of leaving, gives him a kick and knocks the boy down. He struggles to his feet, and he goes away crying.

He meets a cow, and she says, "What's the matter, little boy?"

"*Ay, ay, ay!*" he says. "The little ram knocked me down."

"And why?"

"Because he's in my little chile patch."

"Just wait. I'll go get him out."

The cow comes up, "Moo, moo, moo! Little ram, little ram, get out of that chile patch."

"You big-horned cow, what are you about? Get out of here or I'll kick you out."

"Little ram, little ram, get out of that chile patch."

"You big-horned cow, what are you about? Get out of here or I'll kick you out."

Finally she did try. She tried to hook him with her horns, but the little ram turned around and kicked the cow out.

Then comes the dog, and he says, "I can get him out for sure." And he begins to bark. "Bow-wow-wow-wow! Little ram, little ram, get out of that chile patch."

"You shameless dog, what are you about? Get out of here or I'll kick you out."

"Little ram, little ram, get out of that chile patch."

"You shameless dog, what are you about? Get out of here or I'll kick you out."

The dog kept insisting and he got closer and closer, so the little ram gores him and leaves him the same as the cow.

Then comes the cock. He begins to crow, and he says, "Little ram, little ram, get out of that chile patch."

"You big eared cock, what are you about? Get out of here or I'll kick you out."

Finally the ram gores the cock and leaves him there with his legs in the air, and he goes away.

He kept on eating up the little chile patch, and the boy was very sad because his chile patch was being eaten up. The burro comes, and he says, "Don't worry, little boy, I'll go get the ram out."

The burro begins, "Little ram, little ram, get out of that chile patch."

"You long-eared burro, what are you about? Get out of here or I'll kick you out."

"Little ram, little ram, get out of that chile patch."

"You long-eared burro, what are you about? Get out of here or I'll kick you out."

At last the ram comes up close. He gores the burro and throws him out. And the boy sees that his little chile patch is almost gone, when a little ant comes, and then he says, "Little ant, little ant, if you would get the little ram out of my little chile patch for me, I would give you a lot of corn."

"How much will you give me?"

"I'll give you a bushel."

"That's too much."

"I'll give you half a bushel."

"That's too much."

"I'll give you a *kilo*."

"That's too much."

"I'll give you a handful."

"All right, then."

So the boy went, while the little ant got the ram out, he went and started grinding the corn so the little ant could carry it away without much trouble.

The ant went little by little, little by little, and climbed up one of his little legs. She started to climb, and climb and climb until she got to his little ass.

She stings him and the ram jumps, it leaps and then begins to say, "Oh, my soul, oh, my soul! She has stung me in the hole! Oh, my soul, oh, my soul! She has stung me in the hole!"

And that is how they were able to get the little ram out.

Session Design for "The Ram in the Chile Patch"

Materials

- chiles
- picture or illustration of a ram

Story Drama Activities

1. MOTIVATE children by doing one or more of the following:

   a. Bring several chiles into class and ask students what they are and how they might taste.

   b. Show a picture of a ram and discuss how its horns might be used as a weapon and for protection.

c. Ask children how they might deal with a bully or with someone who steals something from them.

2. PRESENT the story: Students will be asked to develop and improvise a possible resolution to the conflict. Do not reveal the story's ending; stop the telling after the burro has been kicked out of the chile patch. Tell children you will reveal the ending later in the session.

3. DRAMATIZE the story:

a. Inform students the teacher will be playing the role of the ram. Ask the players, "Since I can't really kick you when we work on the story, what can I do to pretend I'm kicking someone?" Negotiate possible solutions with children and incorporate the most playable idea when needed in the dramatization. (In one session the children came up with the idea of the leader stomping his foot on the floor three times as the "signal" for getting kicked.)

b. Ask players how they might show they have been kicked out of the patch without hurting themselves and others. Explore possible solutions with children and incorporate the most playable idea when needed in the dramatization. (Slow motion rolling has been the idea generated most often.) Practice this action sequence—"kicking" and "getting kicked out"—so that all are clear on the process.

c. Ask players to find their own space in the room. Sidecoach them to take on and practice movements for the following roles: "Pretend you're the little boy in the story. Hold on to a hoe or a small shovel and start working on your chile patch. I imagine it might be pretty hot where he lives. Show through your face and body he's working hard in the hot sun." Do not model or demonstrate these actions for children; otherwise, they may simply imitate rather than create their own actions. Sidecoach what you find effective about their work: "Without any sounds, shape your body as if it were a cow. Now let me see through your face and with a soft cow voice how the cow might confront the ram in the chile patch." Share what you find effective about their work and continue this as the remaining animals are created: "Now take on the role of the dog. See how it would be different from the cow you created. Show through your face and a soft dog voice how the dog might confront the ram in the chile patch." Continue with the rooster and the donkey.

d. Distribute the roles among students. The little boy can be played by either one child (boy or girl) or by a small group of three to five children. This decision will be based on whether the teacher feels one child may benefit from playing the individual role, or whether a small group would be best since drama may be new to the class. Once the boy has been cast, divide the remaining roles (cow, dog, rooster, donkey) among the rest of the class so that preferably no more than five children are assigned to each small group.

e. Determine specific "waiting areas" in the classroom for each small group. The ram will be positioned where he can see all students as the teacher interacts with each group of children. Review the rules for the dramatization, which may include: no physical contact; when the signal for being kicked out is given, all should respond appropriately; listen attentively when the teacher is working with one group; etc. The leader should also make certain to announce when he is and is not in role.

f. The child or group playing the boy begins the dramatization by working on the chile patch. The teacher enters as the ram and improvises in role with the boy. Introductory or conflict-generating dialogue might be "Good morning, little boy"; "Mm, these chiles are delicious. I think I'll eat them all up"; "This is *my* patch now, so you'll have to leave." The ram may also wish to incorporate the repetitive phrase "You _____, what are you about? Get out of here or I'll kick you out" just before the end of the unit and the kick. As improvisation is completed with each group, prompt the next group. The teacher may want to ask each group of animals to go to the little boy first to ask what's wrong before coming to the ram. Improvise with the cow, dog, rooster, and donkey. (For assessment purposes, try to keep track of which children improvise freely and which ones remain silent.)

g. After the donkey has been kicked out, drop out of role and bring the class together. Ask, "How are we going to get the ram out of the chile patch?" Discuss possible and playable solutions to the problem. Depending on personal values, violent solutions may be unacceptable. From my personal experience, the solution developed most often by children is collective intimidation toward the ram. Children agree to "gang up" and surround the ram to show there is unity and strength in numbers. Older children sometimes generate the idea of introducing a new character—one much bigger than the ram. When the class agrees on a solution to the problem, the idea is dramatized. The teacher should make certain a satisfying resolution for children is provided by the ram's defeat.

4. ASSESS the dramatization:

a. Offer your observations of effective work from children.

b. Ask players what made it easy to improvise and what made it difficult. If possible, make written notes of which children seem fluent with improvisation and which do not. This can be one criterion for assessing drama work as it continues.

c. Discuss why chiles, a prominent food item in Mexican culture, would be important enough to become an element in a folk story.

d. If interest is high, reveal the "true" ending of the folk tale. I change the resolution by having the ant sting the ram on its *nose*: "After all, how can a ram kick its own nose with its own horns?"

Social Studies Follow-Up

1. Locate Mexico on a globe or map.

2. Discuss how chiles are grown and harvested.

3. Discuss how much a kilo and bushel hold. Compare the measurement systems used in Mexico and the United States.

4. Discuss what countries and governments do when their land is taken or occupied by another country or government. What are the reasons for taking land from or occupying another country? Identify specific events from the past or present.

5. Discuss what a *mercado* is in Hispanic culture. Identify the kinds of items sold there and improvise "a day at the *mercado*" with children playing vendors and customers.

Language Arts/Literature Follow-Up

1. Locate another folktale that uses a repetitive phrase throughout the story, such as "You _____, what are you about? Get out of here or I'll kick you out." Discuss why repetition of an important phrase is used in a story. If the tale lends itself to dramatization, improvise it with the class.

2. An original ending to this story drama was created by the class. Write or tell another possible resolution to the problem for another new ending. Improvise this idea if it lends itself to dramatization.

3. Learn the Spanish language equivalents for the following English words: little, boy, ram, cow, dog, rooster, donkey, ant. Dramatize

the story again, substituting these Spanish words for their English equivalents during the improvised dialogue.

''A Parrot for Christmas''*

This story and its accompanying session design are recommended for grades K–3. Obviously, the drama will be most appropriate before the Christmas holiday season, but I have dramatized this work with children during the summer with "Christmas in July" as the motivating theme. Puppetry is an integral part of the session design, but it is not essential for the story drama.

When retelling this story, the introductory passage on the background of the tale [the first three paragraphs] can be deleted. The storyteller is advised to "sound" like a parrot when reciting the alphabet.

Years ago, while visiting the state of Nayarit, Mexico, I came across a real jungle. It would have been a perfect setting for a Tarzan movie. Large tropical trees with heavy vines interlacing the branches, monkeys peering through the leaves. I got out of the car to have a better look at the wilderness, when, all of a sudden, I found myself surrounded by a flock of parrots. The crackling, the whistling, the chatting were deafening. I was caught in a noisy flying rainbow of yellow, blue and red feathers.

A couple of miles down the road was San Blas, a lazy little village along the Pacific coast. I stopped in a cafe and promptly told a man, who was eating alone at the next table, about my experience in the jungle.

"These parrots are very important to us in San Blas," he said. "Last year, they made the difference between a happy or a sad Christmas for our kids.

Luis Rendón was the envy of all the children in town, last year. His pet parrot, Pepito, was the talk of the town. Pepito followed his master wherever he would go, either perched on his master's shoulder or fluttering around. The parrot even went to school every day.

The kids were learning the alphabet and Pepito had learned his ABCs as well as any of them. One could hear the bird in the streets as the children came out of school 'ABCDEFG.'

Two days before Christmas, disaster struck; towards the end of the

*"A Parrot for Christmas" from *Stories That Must Not Die*, vol. 3, by Juan Sauvageau (Austin, TX: Oasis Press, 1976).

school day a flock of parrots flew by. It was too much for Pepito; he left Luis' shoulder and joined those of his species.

Luis and all his little friends were heart-broken. The Christmas season is no time to be heart-broken. There was no amount of candy and fruit that would make their Christmas a happy one.

For Christmas eve, the teacher had prepared stories and songs and there was going to be a party in the afternoon. The stories did not catch their attention and the children would not sing the songs. What kind of a party would it be with a bunch of sobbing kids?

He decided to help them find Pepito. On their way to the jungle, they met a man who was running towards town. He was very excited. He asked the teacher if some of his pupils were missing. Upon hearing that everybody was accounted for, the man concluded, 'Then there is a new school over there in the jungle because I heard a whole class of children singing the alphabet.'

They ran towards the jungle. They could hear the alphabet very clearly now 'ABCDEFG.' They made their way through the vines and reached a clearing.

The children could hardly contain their excitement when they saw the branches full of parrots. Pepito, like a band director, was leading the other parrots in the reciting of the alphabet.

Luis called Pepito. The parrot came down immediately on his master's shoulder, pecking at his ear gently in order to show how happy he was to be with him again. The other parrots, imitating their new leader, Pepito, came down in a moment. All of a sudden, each child had a parrot of his own, just like Luis.

The kids came back to town and had the greatest Christmas party ever. They sang Christmas carols. The parrots sang the only song they knew, 'ABCDEFG'.''

Session Design for "A Parrot for Christmas"

Materials

- cassette tape of Mexican fiesta music
- cassette tape player
- twelve-inch dowel rods (or popsicle sticks), one for each child
- parrot puppet pattern on white cardstock, one for each child (see illustration at end of session design)
- one assembled (but uncolored) parrot rod puppet
- scissors, one pair for each child
- crayons, markers
- masking or cellophane tape

• photograph or illustration of a parrot
• optional: Mexican parrot rod puppet; available primarily in the south-western U.S. and Mexico

Story Drama Activities

1. MOTIVATE children by doing one or more of the following:

a. Speak Spanish to children in role as an elementary classroom teacher. Improvise such dialogue as *"Buenos dias, niños. Vamos a cantar los ABCs, pero en Ingles."* ("Good morning, children. Let's sing the ABCs, but in English.") Lead the children in the song. Step out of role and ask children "What language was I speaking?" "How did you know that?" "In what countries is Spanish spoken?"

b. If Spanish is a language already used by children in your classroom, show them the Mexican parrot rod puppet, a toy common in the southwestern U.S. and Mexico (if unavailable, use a photograph or illustration of a parrot). Ask questions related to parrots: "In what parts of the world would they be found?" "What do parrots eat?" "Why do you think some parrots have multicolored feathers?"

c. Play the fiesta music on tape. Ask children, "In what country would you hear this music?" If children guess correctly, ask, "How do you know that?"

d. Write the words *Feliz Navidad* on the chalkboard. Ask players, "What language is this?" "What does it mean in English?"

2. PRESENT the story: Children can remain seated at their desks if space is limited while the teacher tells the story. The teacher can walk throughout the classroom during the storytelling.

3. DRAMATIZE the story:

a. Ask children to stand next to their seats. "Without any sounds, shape your body as if it were a parrot." It is preferable if the teacher doesn't model or demonstrate, otherwise children will merely imitate rather than create. "Without any sounds and without disturbing anyone else, walk around your desk/table as if you were a parrot on a tree branch." "Let me offer you a piece of fruit. Without falling, take it in your claw (your foot) and try to put it in your mouth and chew on it." "Now, in a soft voice, repeat what I say but change your voice to sound like a parrot: 'Pretty bird'; 'My name is Pepito'; *'Diga'* ['Talk'].'' (The teacher can improvise other short phrases.) Ask children to be seated. Share what you found effective with their work.

b. Distribute crayons/markers and parrot puppet patterns to each child. Show the assembled but uncolored parrot puppet and ask children to color their own parrots as they wish. Allow time for coloring and play Mexican fiesta music as children are working. When all have completed their work, distribute scissors and have children cut out their puppet patterns. If children are able, have them tape the dowel rods to the back of the puppets with masking or cellophane tape; otherwise, assist children with the assembly. Advise children not to touch anyone else's puppet.

c. Teach children the word *repose*, which means "the puppet at rest." Whenever the teacher says "Repose," all puppets are placed on the desks and hands are taken off the rods. Practice this with the class a few times. Use the control word if children's energies become too scattered with their puppets.

d. All children share their parrot puppet designs with each other. If time is limited, all can sit in a circle with the parrots facing out so everyone can scan each other's work. The teacher can note some of the design choices children may have made for their work such as pastels, primary colors, etc.

e. Have children explore some of the movement possibilities with the parrot puppet. Students, while seated, manipulate the parrot to simulate eating, walking on a branch, and flying. Share what you find effective about their work. (If needed, the first part of the session can be concluded here. Students are to keep their puppets in the classroom until the next session, where they will be used in a dramatization of the story. Ask students to retell the story before the dramatization if the session is continued another day.)

f. Children take on the role of Luis. Ask students to place the parrot puppet on their shoulders as they are taken through the following narrative pantomime: "Gently stroke your hand across Pepito's feathers. Give him a piece of fruit to eat in his beak. Have him gently peck at your ear and it tickles you."

g. Ask children to walk around the room with their puppet against their shoulders as you narrate, "Walk to school. Pretend that other children are looking at you and Pepito and it makes you feel proud to have a parrot as a pet. Walk back to your chair and be seated. I'll pretend to be Luis' teacher and class will begin."

h. The teacher speaks to all children as Luis; improvise other dialogue and questions such as, "Good morning, Luis. I see Pepito is here again today. Hello, Pepito." "Christmas will be here soon. What kind of present are you going to be getting for Pepito?" "What kind of presents do *you* want, Luis?"

i. Continue in role: "Class, yesterday we were learning the alphabet. Everyone did very well, even Pepito. I'd like to hear if Pepito remembers the alphabet song. Pepito, please sing along with me in that parrot voice of yours." The teacher sings the alphabet song; children should sing in their parrot voices. Break out of role, if needed, and ask children to try the song again in parrot voices with the puppets being manipulated to move with each letter.

j. Out of role, explain to the class that they will be dramatizing the part of the story in which Pepito sees a flock of parrots flying overhead and flies away with them. Ask children how this unit might be dramatized, given the limitations of space in the classroom. Negotiate a solution with children and practice it. (The teacher using narrative pantomime might be one solution: "As you walk back home with Pepito on your shoulder, you look up and you see a big flock of parrots flying over you. Pepito starts to flap his wings and flies off your shoulder. Running in place, you try to reach up for him as he's flying away, and you call out to him to come back to you.") Find a place for all puppets to be stored temporarily for the next unit.

k. The teacher explains that students will be playing Luis coming to class the next day, sad that his parrot is lost. Discourage what might be melodramatic crying from some children. The following sidecoaching might be helpful: "Using your face and body only, without any sounds or fake crying, come back to your desk as if you're Luis after he's lost his parrot. Try to show how Luis might be feeling. Begin." Observe and step into role as Luis' teacher.

l. "Good morning Luis. You look sad, what's wrong?" Allow children to improvise dialogue. "Well, I'm sorry to hear about Pepito. But I've planned a Christmas party today and we're going to sing songs and play games; maybe that will make you feel better." If children are committed to the playing, there will be negative responses. Continue in role: "Christmas is no time to be sad. Why don't we go to the jungle together and try to find Pepito? Let's all stand up and get in line. We're going through some dangerous parts of the jungle and I want to make sure I don't lose anybody. Hold hands and I'll lead the way."

m. In a line, take children through the classroom, sidecoaching about the environments you might be going through: "Take high steps when you walk through this tall grass. Duck low to get through these vines. Now be careful and walk slowly through this thick mud."

n. At this point several options for dramatizing the ending of the story may be taken, but if children develop their own idea, use theirs instead:

1. The teacher in role sidecoaches that he hears faint voices that sound like the alphabet song. Suggest that they are the only school in the area. As the group gets closer to the parrot puppets (left in an area of the classroom earlier), the teacher plants the idea that he sees the parrots singing in the tree. Tell children, "Luis, call for Pepito and see if he'll come back down to you." Sidecoach children to call for the parrot; they then get their own rod puppets and place them on their shoulders. Return to the "classroom" and sing a Christmas carol—first as children, then in parrot voices.

2. Step out of role and divide the class into a split-half combination; half will be Luis, the other half will be Pepito (holding on to a puppet created by one of the children playing Luis). If there is an odd number of children, have one child portray the man who asks the teacher if there is another school in the jungle. If an even number of children are present, delete the character from the dramatization. The students portraying the parrots gather together in an area of the classroom to simulate being in a tree. The students portraying Luis walk with the teacher to the tree area. As the children approach the area, the parrot characters grow in volume as they sing the alphabet. On a signal from the teacher, the parrots fly to their designated "master" and improvise dialogue with each other. The teacher brings the class back to the school. All children switch roles and replay the unit.

4. ASSESS the dramatization.

a. Offer your observations of effective work from children. Focus on the players' ability to follow directions.

b. Ask students to describe what they enjoyed most in the dramatization.

c. Ask students how the story might be dramatized if people were used to play the character of Pepito instead of puppets.

Allow children to keep their parrot puppets.

Social Studies Follow-Up

1. Locate the following on a globe or map: Mexico, the Pacific coast of Mexico, Nayarit, San Blas.

2. Discuss how Christmas is celebrated in Mexico. How is it similar to and different from the way Christmas is celebrated in the United

States? Which Mexican Christmas traditions do Mexican Americans maintain in the U.S.? Improvise different "traditional" Christmas mornings for families from different ethnic or cultural backgrounds.

3. Discuss which cultures do not observe Christmas and why.

Language Arts/Literature Follow-Up

1. Locate and read Christmas folk tales from other cultures. Dramatize selected stories through improvisation.

2. Describe the meaning of *envy* (a word used in the story). List and describe other emotions Luis might have experienced. Develop original improvisations based on characters with these emotions.

3. Write or tell an original story about Pepito and Luis set during a different holiday (e.g., Easter, Cinco de Mayo). Play out the story if it lends itself to dramatization.

4. Learn the Spanish-language equivalents for the following English words: jungle, parrot, alphabet, children, school, teacher. Dramatize the story again, substituting these Spanish words for their English equivalents during the improvised dialogue.

5. Retell "A Parrot for Christmas" to a friend or family member, using the parrot puppet when describing the character of Pepito.

"THE POOR WIDOW BULLFIGHTER"*

This is a delightful story for dramatization in grades 3–5. The tale is relatively lengthy and can use judicious editing and summarizing when retelling it for a group of children.

In the story immediately preceding "The Poor Widow Bullfighter" in Brenner's anthology, Florencio, the husband, has been transformed into a bull by an evil priest. This story resumes the action immediately after his disappearance. The magical and benevolent character Tepozton, who helps Mariposa in the story, is the son of a Mexican Indian god. Florencio's adventure is continued after this story; he is transformed back to his human shape when the evil priest is destroyed.

When Florencio disappeared, everybody was sure he was dead. That made his wife a widow. And as her own name was Mariposa, everybody called her the Widow Mariposa.

The worst of it was that she did not know how to support her family. All she could think of was to help her neighbors grind corn. Of course this gave her something to eat, and something to take home for her children too. But she had the oldest, raggedest clothes. And her children, too, could be seen going down the street in rags.

One day she was standing sadly in a cornfield when suddenly she heard a swishing noise. And right in front of her appeared a young man whom she had never seen before. He looked like an ordinary person, but she had never seen an ordinary person appear out of thin air.

"Don't be sad," said this person. "You used to weave pretty sashes and ribbons and girdles. Why don't you make some now, and sell them?"

"I have no wool," said Mariposa.

"I will give you all the wool you want," said the young man. He reached up and reached down, and suddenly Mariposa's hands were full of yarn. There were all the colors of the rainbow.

* "The Poor Widow Bullfighter" from *The Boy Who Could Do Anything & Other Mexican Folk Tales* retold by Anita Brenner (Reading, MA: Addison-Wesley Publishing Co., Inc., 1942 and 1970).

"Oh, thank you! You must be Tepozton," cried Mariposa.

"Yes. Take good care of your children, and don't cry any more." Then Tepozton suddenly wasn't there any more. On the spot where he had been standing, Mariposa saw a lovely green flower beginning to bloom.

So Mariposa made sashes and hair-bands and sold them. She and her children had plenty to eat, and pretty clothes. But one day she got sick. She could not weave any more. Her children were hungry again. Finally Mariposa went to a neighbor's house to grind corn. But she took it home with her so that nobody could see how sick she was.

She worked and worked, and she got so tired that she just sat down and cried. "Oh, if my husband were alive, I wouldn't be suffering like this," she cried. The minute she said that, a very strange thing happened. A big bull walked right into the house.

The bull bellowed, "Quick, quick, close the door." So Mariposa closed the door.

Then the bull said, "Take this rope off my neck and hide it quickly. And if anybody comes here looking for me, say I'm not here." And suddenly he wasn't a bull any more. He was Florencio!

Florencio told Mariposa that he had just run away from the bull ring. They would surely come looking for him. Now that he was a man it was easy to hide him. She rolled him up in a big mat and laid him down in the corner.

Soon a big crowd of people came to the door. "Have you seen a bull around here?"

"Why, no," Mariposa answered. "I haven't noticed a bull or anything like that." They didn't believe her. They saw the print of the bull's hooves inside the door. But they couldn't see a bull any place. They looked in every corner, and behind the door, and under the bed, and one even started to look in the mat that Florencio was rolled up in. But the widow said, "How silly! Who ever heard of a bull being rolled up in a mat?" So they went away.

Florencio came out and kissed his wife and took his children in his arms. He played with them. He stayed a long time. Then the bells in the church began to ring and Florencio started turning back into a bull again. Mariposa cried and cried.

"Now listen," said the bull. "I can't stay with you because I am under a spell. It is Black Magic. But at least I can help you. Tomorrow there is going to be a big bullfight, and I am going to be the third bull in the ring. I will be black all over with white spots on my chest and a white tassel on my tail. And I am going to be very fierce. I won't let anybody get near me. This will tire them out. Then you say that you are going to be a bullfighter. You will show them how. Don't do it too easily.

Take the red cape and wave it and dance around and show them it is hard to do. You will win in the end, and there is a prize of a thousand pesos for the best bullfighter. You can live happily ever after."

"But I am sick," said the Widow Mariposa.

"Don't be silly. Now remember, the third bull, black with white spots on the chest and a white tassel at the end of his tail. Good-by." And he galloped away.

The next day, the Widow Mariposa felt better. She decided to go to the bullfight after all. So she put on her best blue shawl and red petticoat and found herself a seat down in front nearest the bull ring. The first bull that came out was big and black and had white spots on his back. He had a sad and tired look on his face, but he bellowed loudly and tried to look very ferocious. A man went into the ring and threw a lasso around his feet and pulled him down. "That's not the one," said Mariposa.

Now came a bigger, blacker bull with white spots on his head. He pawed the ground and shook his horns and stuck out his tongue and bellowed so loudly that Mariposa put her fingers in her ears and wondered, "Could that be my husband Florencio?"

Everybody was afraid of this bull. It took three men to get him down and they were very proud of themselves. "I guess that's the wrong one too," said Mariposa.

The next bull didn't wait for them to open the gate but crashed right through it so that the splinters flew in all directions. He came in so fast that Mariposa couldn't tell what color he was, and he charged right across the ring and stopped in front of where she was and roared so fiercely that all the other people moved back. But she looked at him and saw the white spots on his chest and a white tassel at the end of his tail and she thought she saw a funny look in his eyes. The men started to fight this bull. The first one who came out danced up to the bull and said, "Huh, huh," but the bull picked him up with the tips of his horns and threw him into Mariposa's lap.

"That is more like Florencio," she said.

Then another man came out and the bull frightened him so much that he ran away and has never been heard of since.

Something happened with every one, until at last the president of the bullfight said, "I guess we'll have to take this bull out. He's too fierce."

"This must be the one," said the Widow Mariposa. So she went up to one of the bullfighters and said, "Please, sir, could I borrow your red cape?"

"What do you want my red cape for?"

"I'm going to play that bull," said the Widow Mariposa.

"How ridiculous! Who ever heard of a woman bullfighter? If you want to make a laughing-stock out of yourself . . . why don't you use your red petticoat?"

The Widow Mariposa then went to the president of the bullfight and said, "Please, sir, would you mind letting me try that bull?"

"But what will you use for a cape?" said the president.

"Why, my red flannel petticoat," said the poor widow bullfighter.

"Ha, ha, ha!" laughed the president. "All right, but everybody will laugh at you. And understand, we are not responsible if the bull kills you, neither can we take charge of the poor innocent children that you leave."

"All right, if the bull kills me I'll be dead," said Mariposa calmly. But she knew that nothing could happen to her because the bull was really Florencio.

So she jumped into the ring and waved her red flannel petticoat. "Ha, ha, ha! Look at the Widow Mariposa! She thinks she's a bullfighter!" everybody cried.

But after a while they stopped laughing. They saw how Mariposa danced around the ring, and the bull roared and ran at her but she dodged him so neatly that nothing happened to her. Finally she took two little spears that were trimmed with colored tissue paper and she waved them at the bull. "Huh, huh, huh!" she grunted, just like a real bullfighter. And the bull bellowed and roared and ran at her, and she stood on her toes and jumped. She landed on his back and rode him all around the ring. The band played and played and everybody clapped.

So Mariposa won the prize for being the best bullfighter. She never had to worry about money again. Everybody called her the Poor Widow Bullfighter, but she really wasn't poor any more.

But a long time afterward, something happened that broke the spell that the wicked priest had put on Florencio. It happened because of a little boy named Chucho.

Session Design for "The Poor Widow Bullfighter"

Materials

- pictures or illustrations of bulls and bullfighters
- four red fabric pieces (for capes)

Story Drama Activities

1. MOTIVATE children by doing one or more of the following:

   a. Show students pictures of bulls and bullfighting from Mexico (or Spain). Discuss the elements of the sport and the spectators' role in the event.

b. Discuss what a widow is and what difficulties she might encounter.

c. Discuss situations or events in which students are "audience members" and "spectators." Ask students to describe differences in audience/spectator behavior when they're at a theatre performance and when they're at a sporting event.

2. PRESENT the story: Retell the story, summarizing those elements at the beginning that are exposition and non-essential to the playing.

3. DRAMATIZE the story:

a. Explain to students that the most playable unit of the story begins when Florencio, as a bull, returns to Mariposa at their home. Select or ask for volunteers to play the following roles: Mariposa, Florencio, and three people investigating the disappearance of a bull. Ensure that those selected will be able to model effective work (e.g., concentration, commitment) for the rest of the class. Talent is not necessarily the only criterion.

b. Discuss the students' roles as audience members when the teacher facilitates the improvisation with the five children. Ask, "What kinds of behaviors are needed by audience members while there's a small group working up here for a short time?" Review and reinforce that respect be exhibited.

c. Ask the two players selected as Mariposa and Florencio to work on the following unit: "Florencio rushes into the house as a bull, then changes into a man and asks Mariposa to hide him. She, of course, is surprised to see him but there's no time to think—she has to act quickly. Since we don't have a mat to roll the character in, what might you use as a hiding place for him?" Solicit ideas from the two students. If the class serving as audience has an idea, ask for their input.

d. Have the students playing the husband and wife improvise the short scene for the rest of the class. Assess the work by sharing with them what the teacher found effective about their work. Then ask the rest of the class, "Mariposa and Florencio were very brave to do this improvisation without any preparation. But since improvisation can always change, what are some things you can offer the two characters to try the second time they do this scene?" Solicit suggestions from the class; ensure that they are constructive suggestions and that there are no specific lines of dialogue they must repeat. Have the two students replay the scene, then assess them on how they incorporated the suggestions.

e. Ask the three students playing the hunters to enter the scene now. Review the scenario they are to enact: they enter and ask if a bull has come by; they search the home; Mariposa does her best to convince them he's not there; the hunters leave. Have them play out the scene; facilitate or sidecoach as needed. Assess what was effective about the work. As before, affirm that the group improvised without any preparation: "Now that they have an opportunity to replay the scene, what suggestions can you offer them?" Solicit and facilitate the replaying, then assess what was effective about their work.

f. Cast and recast (if needed) for the next set of characters in the bullfighting unit: Mariposa, Florencio (as the bull), two other bulls, three matadors, and the president of the bullfight. The bulls, the matadors, and the president do not have to be gender-specific (although the point of the story may be enhanced if the matadors are boys). The rest of the class portrays the spectators at the event.

g. If noise levels in the classroom are a concern, the teacher and class should develop a way for spectators to cheer that will not disturb neighboring classrooms (such as shouts of "¡Ole!" or "¡Andale!" at a whisper, or other nonverbal expressions of praise). Discourage what may be contemporary forms of spectator behavior (e.g., the "wave," chants) to maintain cultural integrity with the piece. If needed, discuss what kinds of spectator behavior might be observed at bullfights.

h. Work with the fight units between the three bulls and matadors; pair each one to the other. (Although the story states that three matadors bring down the second bull, it may be easier to manage the playing by pairing up one bull for each matador and adapting specific actions mentioned in the story.) State at the beginning what behaviors should not be exhibited: "No physical contact is to be made, or we'll have to select someone else who can handle the role responsibly." Demonstrate or "walk through" safe and nondisruptive ways for the bulls and matadors to fight. Use the red fabric pieces as capes. Facilitate the scenes so they are action-specific, perhaps in slow motion. The first matador is triumphant with his bull; the second bull is stronger, is frightening to the crowd, and is tied down by his matador. The third bull, Florencio, enters and gives a signal to Mariposa; after a difficult fight, his matador runs away. Practice this sequence, then replay it with audience cheers. Assess the work the teacher observed, giving particular attention to the students' ability to follow directions and play safely.

i. Have the students playing Mariposa and one of the matadors improvise the unit in which she asks for his cape. Review the scenario, as needed, before they begin. Proceed to the unit where Mariposa and the president of the bullfight improvise their discussion; review the scenario, as needed, before they begin. Emphasize the attitudes that both the matador and president may hold toward Mariposa.

j. Have Mariposa and Florencio, as the bull, stage a bullfight in the center of the room. Mariposa uses a red fabric piece as her cape. Facilitate the playing, emphasizing that Florencio will do everything he can to protect Mariposa. Discuss how the crowd changes their initial attitude toward Mariposa from one of laughter and mockery to one of praise. Play the unit and end the scene by having Mariposa take two imaginary poles and "spear" Florencio. The president improvises his award of a thousand pesos to Mariposa.

4. ASSESS the dramatization:

a. Assess the work observed from students. Share what you observed as their most effective moments and what portions may have needed more commitment or focus.

b. Ask players to share what they enjoyed most about the dramatization. From those who were audience members or spectators, ask what they found effective in those who played a specific character.

c. Discuss the role of the audience member/spectator. Ask students to compare and contrast what makes an effective audience member at a theatre event and at a sporting event.

Social Studies Follow-Up

1. Discuss bullfighting in Mexico. How did it originate? What are some key features of the sport?

2. Discuss how the bullfighting event in Mexico is similar to and different from a contemporary sporting event in the United States. Include a discussion on the participants' and the spectators' roles.

3. Discuss why the men in the story found it so unusual for a woman to bullfight. Also discuss if Mariposa's age may have been a factor in their attitudes toward her ability.

4. Discuss the ethical use and treatment of animals in bullfighting. How might it be viewed from different perspectives in the U.S.? in Mexico? Improvise a scene between animal rights activists and bullfighters on the use of bulls for sport.

Language Arts/Literature Follow-Up

1. Although there are specific tales by Anita Brenner that precede and follow "The Poor Widow Bullfighter," create and write an original "prequel" and/or "sequel" to the given story line. How and why might Florencio have been transformed into a bull? How might the spell have been broken to transform him back into human form? Dramatize these original stories through improvisation.

2. Locate and read folktales from different cultures in which women participate in roles men feel are their domain only. Dramatize these stories through improvisation.

3. Write an original story of a boy or man who is challenged to do a task stereotypically undertaken by a girl or woman. If the story lends itself to dramatization, play it out through improvisation.

"IT'S THE PICHILINGIS AGAIN"

Pichilingis *are mischievous Mexican leprechauns, of sorts. There is no strong story line, per se, in this folktale. It is a collection of incidents about the supernatural pranksters. This story is best used as a springboard for verbal improvisation in grades 3–5. In fact, the session design is geared to introduce children to the dos and don'ts of verbal improvisation and small-group work.*

For this particular story drama the teacher can retell the tale in her own words, but focus more on the description of the pichilingis' pranks than on the portion of the family moving away from their home. Inform the students they will create original stories with the pichilingis.

When my great-grandmother was alive, she would tell of experiences she had had as a young girl living at home with her mother. If they went away for an afternoon, perhaps to visit friends or join a village gathering, the house would be in shambles when they returned. The pichilingis had been up to their mischievous pranks.

The pichilingis could be seen in every place imaginable. You could be walking along a road and suddenly catch a glimpse of one up in a treetop. Sometimes toward evening, you could see them dancing and shouting along the river bed. And at night, while people were sleeping, they would swoop down and drag them off their sleeping mats. The people would wake up at a different place than where they had gone to sleep.

The pichilingis were a nuisance to everyone, but sometimes they would choose a particular family to annoy. My great-grandmother used to tell this story.

There was a family that had somehow attracted the attention of the pichilingis. Every single member of the family was a victim of their pranks. They would be sitting down for a meal with the food on the table ready to eat when suddenly a chunk of mule droppings would fly through the air and land in the beans. Or they would go out to milk the cows in the morning and all they would find was a puddle of milk on the ground. The pichilingis had been at it again.

Needless to say, the family soon reached the point of despair.

"What are we to do?" the wife asked her husband. "Everything is always disappearing. Why, we can't even eat peacefully anymore."

She wanted to leave at once, but her husband was reluctant.

"How can we forsake our house and abandon all our friends?" he wanted to know. "After all, I was born on this ranch."

But the husband, who was also tired of the pichilingis' pranks, finally agreed to leave.

The family packed its belongings and placed them on the burros. Everyone in the community came to see them off. They all knew why the family was leaving.

After a sad farewell, the family started down the road. They traveled all afternoon until it began to get dark. "There's a clearing just ahead," said the husband. "We'll camp here tonight."

In the distance they could see the lights from the campfires. When they finally arrived at the campsite, they unpacked and prepared their dinner. The wife's spirits were high and she prepared a wonderful meal. When they had finished eating it, the husband asked her to make some coffee.

"¡Dios mío!" cried the wife. "I have forgotten the coffeepot."

"It's over here," they heard someone shout.

They turned toward a large mesquite where the voice had come from. To their great surprise, they saw a dozen or so pichilingis sitting around a campfire. The silhouette of the coffeepot flashed with the movement of the fire. All the unfortunate people could do was shake their heads in disbelief and go to sleep.

When they awoke the next morning, they found the coffee pot in the middle of their campfire.

"What's the use of going on?" said the husband. "If the pichilingis are going to be with us, we might as well be at home."

The family packed the burros and started back home.

The pichilingis stayed with the people who lived on the ranchos for many years. But one day, they suddenly went away and never came back.

They went to a mountain called the "Casa Santa."* That's where Noah's Ark is sitting. The pichilingis are the ones that take care of the ark.

They say that a lot of people go to the mountain to visit. You can go inside, but if you have evil thoughts or if you steal something, the pichilingis won't let you out again.

Session Design for "It's the Pichilingis Again"

Materials

- art paper
- crayons/markers

Story Drama Activities

1. MOTIVATE children by doing one or more of the following:

a. Before children enter the room, purposefully create a disarrayed atmosphere (chairs piled together in a corner, papers strewn about the floor, upside down pictures and letters on a bulletin board, etc.). Write in large letters on the chalkboard such messages as, "THE PICHILINGIS WERE HERE." When children enter the room, ask if they know who the pichilingis are and why the room is a mess.

b. Discuss why, when things go wrong, strange accidents happen, or items are suddenly missing, people might blame the event on some outside force rather than human intervention.

c. Discuss the advantages of problem solving by group effort rather than by oneself.

2. PRESENT the story: Focus on the pichilingis' pranks rather than the telling of a story with a beginning, middle, and end. The purpose of the presentation is to acquaint students with this culturally specific folk character and the personality traits inferred from its actions.

3. DRAMATIZE the story: (There is a great amount of preparatory discussion in the session design, but it is an investment in time that will reap benefits for future drama work.)

a. Ask players to get into groups of three to five (if the teacher feels comfortable with students grouping themselves; if not, the teacher

* Holy House

can make decisions for group composition, or have groups formed by students "counting off" from one to five).

b. When groups are formed and gathered, tell students what their task will be: "You and your group members will be developing a two- to three-minute verbal improvisation to share with the rest of the class. The scenario will include the pichilingis as characters, and the conflict will be the problem a group of humans encounters when the pichilingis play a trick on them. What were some of the tricks you heard in the story?" Have students recall specific incidents. "Now let's think about what other kinds of tricks might be played by the pichilingis. What are some tricks that you didn't hear in the story?" Solicit ideas from children.

c. Discuss the process of small-group work: "Before I let you get to work, we need to discuss and agree on some ways group decisions get made for improvisation. First, what kinds of decisions are you and your group going to have to make to develop and show the improvisation?" The teacher solicits ideas from the class and notes other points which may not get raised; for example, the group will have to

1. discuss ideas for a scenario, then select the one that is the most playable;

2. refine the story line so it has a definite beginning, middle, and end;

3. decide who is going to play which character;

4. decide what kind of space or furniture may be needed for the improvisation;

5. practice (not just talk about) the improvisation several times and decide what changes need to be made to make the scenario or improvisation work more effectively.

d. Discuss with the class what dynamics will make a group work effectively. Solicit ideas from the class and mention points not raised; for example, the group members should

1. listen to each other's ideas openly without judgment during the discussion; provide an example of what is open acceptance ("OK, that's one idea. Any others?") and what is not ("No, that's a stupid idea.");

2. agree on the scenario for the improvisation; if only one or two people are not in agreement with the others they should be willing

to go with the majority decision for the initial practice of the
improvisation;

3. be satisfied with the character each member would like play in
the improvisation but be willing to play a different character if
needed;

4. concentrate during practice periods for the improvisation;

5. assess the initial practice of the improvisation honestly with the
rest of the group ("I think we can do better if we . . .") but
without condemnation or overt direction ("You shouldn't have
said that line, that was wrong.").

e. Discuss some common problems that might occur in group work
and ask students to make suggestions for resolution. For example,
ask what students should do in their groups if
1. one person tries to "take charge" of the group;

2. one person won't agree to the decisions of the group and refuses
to take part in the improvisation;

3. one person is reluctant or hesitant about participating;

4. one person becomes or is seen as the "outcast" of the group.

f. Discuss verbal improvisation (see Chapter One) and its demands for
a player in drama. Discuss what makes an effective improvisation (a
strong conflict; concentration on the task; people who can be heard
by others; a definite beginning, middle, and end; etc.) and what
makes an ineffective improvisation (the opposite of the points mentioned above: no conflict to the scenario; people who are not concentrating on the task; people speaking softly or not at all; no clear
beginning, middle, or end; etc.). Write points mentioned on the
chalkboard for reinforcement.

g. Review the initial group task and introduce a new charge: "You and
your group members will be developing a two- to three-minute
improvisation to share with the rest of the class. The scenario will
include the pichilingis as characters, and the conflict will be the
problem a group of humans encounters when the pichilingis play a
trick on them. You can dramatize one of the tricks you heard in the
story, one of the original tricks we discussed earlier, or come up with
a brand new one. I want you to practice all the things we've discussed
about making a group work effectively, but here's a strange thing I
want you to do with the improvisation when you share it with the
rest of the class. Deliberately make the improvisation bad. Dramatize

your scenario so the work we see you do shows us all the things that make an improvisation ineffective. That seems like a strange thing to do after we discussed what makes a good improvisation, but here's why: You won't be able to do your best until you know what your worst can be. I want you to experience what it's like to share ineffective work so you'll never have to do it again. Each group will share their bad improvisation. Then we'll talk about the specific things we saw that went wrong. You'll go back to your groups to practice the improvisations, but you'll be practicing to make them the best they can be. But for now, you and your groups have a lot of work to do in ten minutes to develop and practice a bad two- to three-minute improvisation. Any questions? [answer, as needed] Go to work. I'll help you if you need it."

The hidden agenda behind the deliberate request for bad work is to allay the fears of a class's first effort at verbal improvisation. Most initial efforts *will* be "bad" or ineffective, since independent group work is difficult. Students might experience a sense of success if the quality of their work matches the teacher's expectations.

h. As groups work, the teacher goes from group to group and assists. After ten minutes (shorter or longer, as needed) gather everyone's attention: "I know you've had just a short time to practice, but that's all right. Remember, what we want to see is a bad improvisation." Solicit volunteers for the group that will go first, second, third, etc., and write the list on the chalkboard.

i. Have each group share their improvisation in front of the class. After each group shares, ask the class to point out what things were done deliberately to make the improvisation ineffective. Praise the groups for their "bad" work since that was the point of the improvisation.

j. Provide directions for the next unit: "Now your group's task is to practice your improvisation again, only this time we want you to make it as good as it can be. You've already done your worst; now we want you to do your best. Concentrate, help each other, listen to what other characters are saying—do everything you can to make your scene effective. You'll have about ten minutes to work, then you'll share your improvisations with the rest of the class. Any questions? [answer, as needed] Go to work. I'll help you if you need it."

k. As players work, the teacher goes from group to group and assists, as needed. After ten minutes (shorter or longer, as needed) gather everyone's attention: "Now we'll see the best work you and your group are able to do with the pichilingis improvisation. We'll see the groups in the same order as the first set."

4. ASSESS the dramatization:

a. After each group shares, the leader and class point out what things were done differently to make the improvisations more effective.

b. Ask players to review group dynamics that make for effective group process.

c. Ask players to share what decisions or problems might have been encountered in their groups and what steps were taken, if any, to solve them.

d. Distribute art paper and crayons/markers. Ask students to draw what they think a pichilingi looks like. Display the art work. (If a writing activity is preferred, see the Language Arts/Literature Follow-Up, below.)

Social Studies Follow-Up

1. Locate Mexico on a globe or map.

2. Discuss where the remains of Noah's Ark are believed to be located. Locate this landmark on a globe or map. Develop and improvise a scene in which explorers encounter pichilingis at the remains of Noah's Ark.

3. Discuss why some cultures' folklore includes a mischievous or trickster character. Speculate why different cultures would develop their own unique folk characters that share this mischievous or trickster personality trait.

4. Discuss the principles of a democracy and how the small group functions in a democratic manner.

Language Arts/Literature Follow-Up

1. Write or tell an original story (not shown in a group improvisation) about the pichilingis. Dramatize the story through improvisation.

2. Script the improvisation that was developed by a group into a standard play format (with stage directions, entrances and exits, etc.).

3. This story was passed down from a relative of Campos. Ask older family members (parent, grandparent, aunt/uncle) to tell you a story or a legend told to them by another family member. Practice retelling the story, then tell it to someone else in your family or to a friend

in class. If some of these stories lend themselves to dramatization, play them out in class.

4. Read stories from other cultures that have mischievous or trickster characters (e.g., the leprechaun from Ireland, Anansi from Africa, Coyote from several Native American tribes). Dramatize stories that lend themselves to improvisation.

"THE WEEPING WOMAN" (*La llorona*)

This story is geared for grades 5–6 and can be used with the secondary school grade levels as well. The session design is tailored for small-group work.

A canon of Mexican and Mexican American folklore would be incomplete without this melodramatic story. It is the most well-known tale among the culture. It is also a violent story. Sadly, the events leading to the main character's actions and death are all too possible in today's world. This may be why the story drama is successful with older children and adolescents. There are parallels to their own lives, particularly with the large number of single parent homes and high divorce rate among families. Teachers should not be afraid to explore such life issues with their children as school and community standards allow. The story drama requires tremendous concentration and commitment from children. If played well, it can be a powerful experience.

Ay, pity poor Luisa. Back in the fifties life in the *barrio* with her three little children was not easy. Her husband, that low-life *borracho*, spent all his time in the *cantinas* of Nuevo Laredo, leaving his family to fend for themselves in their miserable little home.

Luisa would always put her children first, feeding them whatever she could while she herself went hungry day after day. To make money, she washed and ironed clothes for some of the White ladies in Laredo. But Luisa grew tired and could only do so much, ¿*tú sabes*? Since they paid little for her labor, Luisa even had to beg for money in the streets. A few would offer whatever they could, but most ignored her or thought her a liar. And this was her life, *pobrecita*, hard and cold.

One day after having been gone for weeks, Luisa's husband returned. The children rushed to their father, happy to see him, but Luisa kept back and said nothing. She prayed silently that this time, this time, he would stay for good—but that was not to be. He had fallen in love with another woman who lived across the border. So he told his family goodbye, packed his clothes, and left.

Luisa stood silent while the children cried around her. The shock dried her throat and she turned pale as a ghost. What was she going to do now? How could she take care of her children?

We try to go on, no matter what—but it's hard, *¿verdad?*

Luisa became poorer and more tired as time went by. And her eyes became emptier, which frightened the children. Poor *niños*—no food to eat and a mother half gone from this world.

One night she and her little ones were walking along the Rio Grande after a special mass. Luisa gazed at the water and saw the moon and stars dancing on the surface. Then she looked at the sky and thought that her children would be better off in heaven: "They'll be angels with God and never know misery again."

Luisa hugged her children tightly, tightly, then pushed them into the river to drown. *¡Asesina!* She waited until she couldn't hear or see them, then turned and walked away. Luisa returned home, crawled into her bed, and pulled the blanket over her. "They're with God now," she thought to herself, and closed her eyes to rest.

Luisa awoke in the middle of the night and felt like she had been reborn. She stretched, smiled, and walked to her children's bedroom to gaze at them while they slept, but there was only an empty mattress on the floor. Then the memory and tragedy of what she had done came upon her and she screamed in agony, "No!"

She ran along the river's edge, crying and searching desperately for her babies. "*Ay, Dios mío,*" she whispered through her sobbing, "What have I done? What have I done?" The moon and the stars danced on the river's surface. Luisa looked into the water and saw what she thought were her own dear children reaching up to her for help. She cried in joy and threw herself into the river to rescue them. . . .

Ay, pity poor Luisa. She, too, drowned in the waters of the Rio Grande.

They say if you're by a river at night, you might hear what sounds like a weeping woman along the banks. Some say it's the wind; others say it's the water. But some say it's the ghost of Luisa, *La llorona,* still crying and looking for her children to this day.

Special Vocabulary

- *barrio* - neighborhood (usually poor)
- *borracho* - drunkard
- *cantinas* - bars
- *¿tú sabes?* - you know?

- *pobrecita* - poor thing (fem.)
- *¿verdad?* - true?
- *niños* - children
- *asesina* - murderer (fem.)
- *Dios mío* - my God

Session Design for "The Weeping Woman" (*La llorona*)

Materials

- cassette tape recording of mood music (somber, solemn, minor keys) ("La llorona" is a folk melody from Mexico and may be found in some collections of music from the country)
- cassette tape player
- optional: black pieces of fabric (assorted lengths and sizes), adaptable as shawls, hoods, skirts, capes, scarves, headbands.

Story Drama Activities

1. MOTIVATE children by doing one or more of the following:

a. Discuss the difficulty of dramatizing serious material in class. Ask students what challenges are faced and what demands are required of them to make the drama effective.

b. Ask, "What would make a mother murder her children? What reasons could she possibly have for killing them?" Facilitate the discussion.

c. Ask students to describe what life in a *barrio* is like. Ask what kinds of people and conditions would be found in a *barrio*.

d. Show pieces of black fabric and ask students what emotions or symbolic representations the color may evoke.

e. Briefly retell the myth of Medea, whose husband (Jason) left her for another woman. Out of revenge, Medea killed the children she and Jason bore. Euripides, the Greek playwright, wrote a play about this character and developed one of the most powerful lines of dialogue in dramatic literature. When Jason cries in agony and asks Medea why she murdered their children, she hisses back, "Because I hated you more than I loved them." Segue into the presentation by sharing how this myth has parallels to a tale from Hispanic culture.

2. PRESENT the story: The leader should model for students the serious tone needed for the dramatization by retelling the tale with dignity and simplicity. There is no need to make this a "ghost story." It is a tragic tale whose actions could very likely happen today.

3. DRAMATIZE the story:

a. Since this story and session design are geared for upper elementary students, discuss the importance of everyone playing the same key role from the story regardless of gender: "One purpose of the dramatization is to understand the character's emotions and motivations for action. So having everyone play the role of Luisa may provide some insights you might not get by simply watching other people's work." Mention that when we feel uncomfortable with a particular situation we sometimes try to "laugh it off." Challenge students to commit to the seriousness of the work and to be honest with their actions.

b. If possible, dim the lights in the room for a more comfortable and secure space for mood pantomime. Mood music played softly will also support the children's work. Ask students to find their own space. Tell players to "Choose one of the actions Luisa might be doing daily: ironing or washing clothes by hand, preparing food, begging for money. Try to image in your mind the emotions or physical state this character might be experiencing as she's doing one of these tasks. Maybe she's ashamed to beg, exhausted as she's ironing, or hungry as she's preparing food because it's for her children only and not for herself. Don't be afraid to try a couple of ideas, and don't worry about what anybody else is doing. Work for yourself and by yourself. Begin." Observe the players' work. Sidecoach, as needed, if students appear hesitant to participate or seem uncommitted: "If you're stuck for an idea or find this hard to do, pretend you're begging me for money to feed your children and show through your face and body that you're trying to get my sympathy. As I walk around the room, try to catch my eye and make me feel as if I should offer you something." Walk around the space and interact with players; praise effective work and continue to sidecoach. If desired, the leader can prompt: "Keep working. I'm going to tap some of you on the shoulder. Verbalize a phrase or sentence that represents what Luisa might be thinking or feeling at this time." Select a few or all players to respond. Ask players to relax and reassemble the students.

c. Discuss with players the ease or difficulty of committing to the unit above. As students raise difficulties, the teacher should offer suggestions or find specific ways to help them concentrate on their work.

d. Students are now divided into groups of various sizes. The scenario outline below describes the number of players required for each unit, casting suggestions, and the unit of action each group is to dramatize.

Facilitate the organization of the groups. Having each unit scenario on a separate sheet of paper for the players will save time verbally describing each group's task. Since unit four is particularly difficult to dramatize because of the seriousness and intense commitment needed on the part of the players, the teacher may wish to select students (by teacher assignments or student volunteers) for this particular one first. After this unit has been cast, the remaining ones can be assigned to the remainder of the class. When "extras" are mentioned in units three and six, the number of students required is flexible to accommodate the number of students in the class. There are seventeen opportunities to play a specific role (one for a boy, seven for girls, and nine for the children). Keeping the genders of the children consistent from one unit to the next may not be necessary but may provide believability as the scenes are shared. (The unit contents are suggested by the action of the story itself. Some classes with which I've worked have added other units, such as a scene between Luisa and a priest. Depending on the number of students and the flexibility of the teacher, other units that relate to the story or elaborate on the action can be added. An optional unit between units five and six is included if one girl feels comfortable doing solo work.)

1. UNIT ONE CAST: one girl (Luisa), three of either gender (the children)

   SCENARIO: Develop a scene in which we first see the mother (Luisa) with her three children. Set the scene at their home, perhaps during a meal. Show how their poor existence makes life difficult for them. Mention how the father has not been home for several days. End the unit with the children sent to bed, leaving Luisa alone.

2. UNIT TWO CAST: two girls (one as Luisa, one as a woman for whom she does laundry)

   SCENARIO: Develop a scene in which Luisa delivers clean laundry to the woman's home. Have the two converse about Luisa's problems with her family. End the unit with the woman expressing sympathy but being unable to help Luisa.

3. UNIT THREE CAST: one girl (Luisa), extras (a flexible number of either gender)

   SCENARIO: Develop a scene in which Luisa begs for food and money in the street. Show several passersby as individuals or couples reacting to, talking with, or ignoring Luisa. End the unit with Luisa leaving for home after all passersby have interacted with her.

4. UNIT FOUR CAST: one boy (Luisa's husband), one girl (Luisa), and three of either gender (the children)

SCENARIO: Develop a scene in which Luisa's husband returns home after a long absence. After an uncomfortable and awkward time, he tells Luisa he is leaving her and the children for another woman. Through pantomime and verbal improvisation, show how each family member reacts and feels. End the unit with the husband leaving.

5. UNIT FIVE CAST: one girl (Luisa), three of either gender (the children)

SCENARIO: Develop a scene in which Luisa and her children are walking along the river. Improvise what the family might be discussing at this moment of the story. Dramatize the moment in which Luisa hugs her children and pushes them into the river. End the unit with Luisa leaving for home.

[(OPTIONAL UNIT CAST: one girl (Luisa)

OPTIONAL UNIT SCENARIO: Develop a scene in which Luisa wakes up after she has killed her children. Dramatize the moments she sees the empty bed, runs to the river to look for her children, and throws herself into the Rio Grande.]

6. UNIT SIX CAST: one girl (La llorona), extras (as modern-day youth)

SCENARIO: Develop a scene in which young people are by the river at night. Set the scene in the present; suggest that the environment is eerie. La llorona's crying is heard, but since no one is seen the youth are scared off. End the scene with La llorona walking along the banks of the river looking for her children.

e. After groups have been organized and the scenarios distributed, review the guidelines for practicing and sharing: "Some of the most important things to do are to focus on the work, to make it believable, and not to fall into the trap of trying to be funny or laughing something off. You and your group have about fifteen to twenty minutes to develop these scenarios through improvised dialogue. What you share with the rest of the class should last about two to three minutes. Don't just talk about what you're going to do and say; get on your feet and actually go through the improvisation a few times. That way, you'll feel more comfortable about your work. If you need to use some of the chairs in the room for your scene, go ahead and do so. When we share these units, they'll be presented in the order they occur in the story. Any questions? [answer, as needed] Then let's get to work."

f. If the leader anticipates that generating dialogue would be extremely difficult for the group, an alternative to the dramatization may be to ask for tableaus—frozen, carefully composed arrangements of people in a group whose placement, postures, facial expressions, and other visual details capsulize the meaning or emotional intent of the unit. Once the group has successfully completed and shared these tableaus, dialogue could be integrated with a replaying.

g. If the fabric pieces are used, share with the group, "There are also some black pieces of fabric that can be worked into the scene as tablecloths, shawls, veils, capes, scarves, wraparound skirts, many different things. Try to incorporate at least one piece into your group as a costume accessory or a scenic element to lend some unity to the whole dramatization when we put it together."

h. The teacher goes from group to group assessing progress and assisting, as needed. After time allocated for the practice period, gather the class together and review the order of presentations. Also give one final suggestion: "When your group is finished with the improvisation, don't tell us in any way that the scene is over. One of the worst ways to end what could be an exciting scene is to finish the last line of dialogue, then to break the mood you might have created by turning to us and saying, 'That's it.' The best thing to do is to freeze the action in your scene, then walk slowly away from the area. That will be the cue for the next group to begin their scene." Organize the groups in their order of presentations around the room. Review any last-minute guidelines (laughter, concentration, etc.). If possible, keep the lights dimmed in the room to enhance concentration and establish mood. Facilitate the presentation of each group's unit.

4. **ASSESS the dramatization:**
   a. Ask students to share what they found effective about their own work, their group's work, and others' work. The teacher offers her observations to the class on what she found effective.

   b. Discuss the commitment achieved from students during the improvisation. Ask students what techniques or strategies they employed to focus on their work. If the commitment was not always present, what were the reasons for losing concentration? Relate how an actor on stage, television, or film might need this same kind of commitment for performance.

   c. Discuss the character of Luisa. Ask students what new insights they may have made into her motivations for action.

d. Discuss how the class might reorganize the dramatization to allow, with continuous practice, development of the story into a finished product for performance.

e. If fabric pieces were used, discuss how the use of them contributed to the visual look of the dramatization. Discuss how this might transfer to a stage by a scenic and costume designer.

Social Studies Follow-Up

1. Locate Laredo (Texas), Nuevo Laredo (Mexico), and the Rio Grande on a globe or map.

2. Survey people of Hispanic descent and ask if they have heard or know the story of "La llorona." Survey people from a different cultural background (White, African American) and ask the same question. Draw an inference from the results. (Note: "La llorona" may be more well known in the southwestern U.S.)

3. Discuss the character of Luisa from a cultural and feminist perspective. What is her role as a woman defined by traditional Hispanic culture? What actions in the story support this? How might Luisa be seen from a feminist point of view?

4. The problems and actions of Luisa are all too possible in today's world. Discuss what social institutions and agencies are in place today that might help someone with Luisa's problems to prevent these tragic events from occurring.

Language Arts/Literature Follow-Up

1. Read the Greek myth of Medea. Compare and contrast the Greek tale with "The Weeping Woman." Discuss how Medea's and Luisa's problems and motivations for their actions are similar and different. Dramatize the myth through improvisation.

2. This version of "The Weeping Woman" integrates a few Spanish words into the English text. "Spanglish" is a slang term for this language combination. Discuss why people who know both languages might combine words and phrases from both English and Spanish when speaking in everyday conversation.

3. Ask two Hispanics who know the story of "La llorona" to retell it for you, and record each one's story on audiotape. Ask how or where they first heard the tale. Transcribe their stories and the interviews.

Write a report that discusses the similarities and differences between their versions of the tale. Discuss why the similarities and differences are present.

4. Transform the verbal improvisation into a play by writing the dialogue as a scripted work.

4

Stories from the Native American Canons

"Why Bears Have Short Tails"

This legend is easily dramatized by grades K–4 children. It is suitable as beginning material for those groups with little or no drama experience. The leader plays in role as the Fox while children portray the Bear.

Byrd Baylor collected the stories for her anthology from Native American children in Arizona. This story is told in the child's own words.

Fox was fishing in the river. When he had ten fish he put them on his back and walked off into the woods.

Bear came along and saw Fox with the fish on his back.

"How come you have so many fishes on your back? How are you fishing those fishes out of the water?"

Fox said, "It's easy. You sit on the ice and put your tail in the river. The fishes catch onto your tail and when you get up there will be all of those fishes just hanging on."

"Thanks," said Bear as he ran off toward the river. He didn't know Fox was laughing as he went along through the woods with his ten fish.

Bear sat on the ice. He sat there a long time, waiting and waiting. He didn't notice any fish jumping onto his tail. All he noticed was that his tail was freezing. It hurt.

After a long time, Bear said, "I can't feel my tail."

He got up and looked. It was true. His long tail had frozen off. All he had left was a very short tail.

Bear was angry. He gave up fishing and ran into the woods looking for Fox.

Fox was cooking his ten fish when Bear grabbed him.

Bear said, "You tricked me and my beautiful long tail froze off. So now I'm taking you back to that river. I'll throw you in and let you freeze."

"No," Fox said. "Don't do that. If you let me go I'll give you all my fish."

So Bear let Fox go and ate all the fish himself and warmed his short tail by Fox's fire.

Now all bears have short tails. That is how it happened.

Sandra Begay
Navajo
Tuba City Boarding School

Session Design for "Why Bears Have Short Tails"

Materials

- illustrations of a fox and a bear

Story Drama Activities

1. MOTIVATE children by doing one or more of the following:
a. Show illustrations of a fox and a bear. Ask children to describe their similarities and differences; mention the differences between their tails.

b. Ask players what might happen if a popsicle stick is abruptly removed from a frozen popsicle, or if a stem is removed quickly from an apple. Use this discussion to segue into the story.

2. PRESENT the story: A straightforward retelling of this brief tale is sufficient.

3. DRAMATIZE the story:
a. Ask players to find their own space in the room. "Shape your body as if you were pretending to be a bear. Think about how it might walk on the ground and begin moving slowly around the space." Observe players' work and sidecoach, as needed. "I'm going to pretend to be Fox fishing in the river. Without getting behind anything in the room, try to show you're hiding behind a tree watching me. When I gather all of my fish, step out from behind your tree

and we'll talk." The leader, as the Fox, pretends to catch fish from the river with her paws and teeth. Observe children as they "hide."

b. Enter the center of the space as the Fox. If children do not initiate dialogue the leader might begin with an introductory line such as, "Bear, is that you behind the tree?" Improvise with children according to the exchange in the story. (It is not essential that the dialogue be replicated exactly as it was retold.) The leader responds to those children who may be initiating dialogue. If she would like certain children to have the opportunity to improvise she can ask children who are silent such questions as, "Do you think you can eat all ten fish by yourself?" or "What other things besides fish do you eat?" The leader may also want to assume such characteristics in vocal tone as slyness and deception for the Fox. After the leader feels a suitable amount of dialogue has been exchanged, she may proceed into the next unit, telling the Bears to dip their tails in the water and wait for the fish to come.

c. The leader drops out of role and sidecoaches to children: "I'm not the Fox anymore. Walk over to your own space that will be the river bank. Dip your long tail into the cold water and show through your face and body how Bear might react to that. It's a little uncomfortable, but think about all the fish you're going to catch. After waiting for a long time you start to get colder and you try to do things to stay warm." Observe children as they work; reinforce effective actions. "After waiting all day in the cold you start thinking that maybe Fox wasn't being truthful with you, and you start to softly, quietly get a little upset. You decide to go have a word with Fox and you try to get up, but you're stuck. You try pulling and pulling but you're stuck. Look behind you and see that your tail's frozen in the water. Try to pull . . . pull . . . and you're out. Look behind you and see that your beautiful long tail is stuck in the frozen river. Think about how Bear might feel and start walking slowly and silently around the space, thinking to yourself how you've been tricked. I'm going to come back into the playing as the Fox. Let's see what kind of conversation they have. Remember to respect each other's space, so no physical contact."

d. The leader initiates the dialogue as she enters the action: "Hello, Bear. Did you catch any fish?" Improvise with children as they dialogue with the leader. Rather than acquiesce quickly to their demands for the fish, the leader might choose to extend the dialogue by asking them questions, such as "How long were you waiting in the river?" "Why didn't you just wait for the ice to melt?" When the leader senses enough dialogue has been exchanged, and Bear's threats have become the strongest, she offers Bear the fish and asks players to sit down by the fire to warm themselves.

4. ASSESS the dramatization:

a. Discuss the emotions the Bear might have experienced in the story as children portrayed them. Extend beyond the basic descriptions of "mad" and explore when Bear might have felt "foolish," "worried," "satisfied," etc. Ask players what emotions or thoughts might have been been running through Fox's mind as she talked with Bear at the beginning and end of the story.

b. Share with players what the leader observed about their verbal improvisation. Assess their fluency with language, the appropriateness of their dialogue for the character, and their ability to respond to leader questioning. Praise effective work as well.

c. Assess the children's nonverbal work, particularly as they were portraying the Bear by the river.

Social Studies Follow-Up

1. This same story has been documented in the Cherokee canon of legends. Locate on a map where the Dine (Navajo) and Cherokee nations are located. Discuss how and why this story is present in the two tribes' story canons.

2. This same story has also been found in the folklore canon of Norway. Discuss how and why this story is present in two areas (Arizona and Norway) with such wide geographical distance between them.

3. Discuss what kinds of climate and natural environment are needed for this story's action to occur. Discuss how geography and environment might influence the development and content of a story or legend.

Language Arts/Literature Follow-Up

1. Discuss the characters of Fox and Bear. Write lists of adjectives that describe each one's physical characteristics and personalities. Dramatize the story again with children as Fox and the leader as Bear.

2. Discuss the difference between *dialogue* and *narration*. Identify which portions in the story are dialogue and which portions are narration.

3. Read other "why" or "how" stories from the Native American canons. Discuss why all cultures have developed these types of stories

to explain why or how things came to be. Dramatize those tales that lend themselves to improvisation.

"The Medicine Man"

This story for grades K–4 features one of the most prominent characters in Native American stories: Coyote. Coyote is generally seen as a comic figure who continually gets into trouble of one kind or another. "The Medicine Man" is an excellent story that summarizes his general characteristics: sometimes well-meaning, sometimes foolish, often in trouble, but always surviving.

The session design for this story uses primarily narrative pantomime to explore the characters and provides opportunities for brief exchanges of dialogue. It is suitable as beginning material for those groups with little or no drama experience.

There is a telling that, in the beginning, when the animals first came up from the darkness to live above the ground, Coyote was sent ahead by Thought Woman to carry a buckskin pouch far to the south.

"You must be very careful not to open the pouch," she told him, "or you will be punished."

For many days, Coyote ran southward with the pouch on his back. But the world was new, and there was nothing to eat along the way, so he grew very hungry. He wondered if there might be food in the pouch. At last, he took it from his back and untied the thongs. He looked inside and saw nothing but stars. Of course, as soon as the pouch was opened, the stars all flew up into the sky, and there they are to this day.

"Now look what you've done," said Thought Woman. "For now you shall always get into trouble everywhere you go."

And because Coyote disobeyed, he was also made to suffer with the toothache. When the other animals were asleep, he could only sit and howl at the stars. Thus, he has been crying ever since the beginning of the world.

Sometimes he would ask the other animals to cure him, but they would only catch the toothache from him, and they, too, would cry.

One day, he met Mouse, who lived in a little mound under the chaparral bush. "Friend Mouse," begged Coyote, "can you cure me of this toothache?"

Now it happened that while digging underground, as is his habit, Mouse had come upon a sweet-smelling root and had put it with the other herbs in the pouch he always carried. He was said to be very wise in the use of herbs.

"I don't know," said Mouse, "but I have just found a new root, and it may be that it will help you." He rubbed the root on Coyote's swollen cheek, and in a little while the toothache was gone.

This is how it happened that coyotes never hunt or kill field mice.

This story from Coyote Tales from the Indian Pueblos *by Evelyn Dahl Reed [1991] appears courtesy of Sunstone Press, Box 2321, Santa Fe, NM 87504-2321.*

Session Design for "The Medicine Man"

Materials

- leather pouch
- cassette tape player
- cassette tape of contemporary Native American flute music

Story Drama Activities

1. MOTIVATE children by doing one or more of the following:

a. Show students a leather pouch and ask them how stars might be contained within it.

b. Ask students what past cultures might have done for toothaches before modern dentistry.

c. Ask players, "Why does a coyote howl?"

d. Ask players what they know about the role of the medicine man in some Native American cultures.

2. PRESENT the story: A straightforward telling of this simple tale is all that is needed. The leader should not be reluctant to howl like a coyote, when appropriate.

3. DRAMATIZE the story: (The session design will be described with gender-specific roles, although it is not essential that this prescribed casting be followed.)

a. The character of Thought Woman is an intriguing one to re-create.[1] Split-half casting with girls as Thought Woman and boys as Coyote may be appropriate for the first playing. If possible, dim the lights

---

1.   An excellent leader reference for learning more about Thought Woman is Paula Gunn Allen's *The Sacred Hoop* [Boston: Beacon Press, 1992, 11–29].

in the room and play contemporary Native American flute music softly. Ask players to partner up by boy and girl. If there is an uneven mix, some children may be grouped in threes, as needed (e.g., one Thought Woman for two Coyotes). Younger players may protest this mixed-gender grouping. Assure them it is essential for the dramatization and, to use a female colleague's response when she encounters this problem, say, "You don't have to marry each other, just work with each other."

b. Boys are off to the side observing while girls are in the center of the room, each in her own space. The leader sidecoaches: "Imagine what it would be like to portray Thought Woman, a powerful spirit and creator. Walk through the space as if you're looking at the world and the universe around you as it exists for now. Explore how Thought Woman might move around the space and how it might be different from the way you walk every day. Take a look at the things that have been created so far on the earth and what seems to be missing. You come up with an idea for light, so you take a leather pouch and you put some bits of light inside it and close it tightly. Now you need someone to take the light where it needs to go." Ask players to relax and be seated. Assess the work with emphasis on movement created for Thought Woman. Ask boys to enter the playing space while girls observe at the side.

c. Ask boys to shape their bodies to look like a coyote; mention that being on all fours is not essential as long as a sense of character is displayed in an upright position. Ask them to "silently and without touching anybody else or worrying about what anybody else is doing, move around the space as Coyote, looking at the things that have been created in the world so far. There's no food, though, and you're a little hungry, so you search for something to eat. But there's nothing around." Ask players to relax and be seated. Assess the work with emphasis on movement created for Coyote.

d. The girls, as Thought Women, are instructed to approach their Coyote partners, give them the pouch, and tell them to take it south. "Thought Women, don't forget to warn Coyote about keeping the pouch closed. Coyotes, Thought Women are powerful and are to be treated with respect. Thought Women, when you've finished giving your instructions to Coyote, return to the side. Begin." Observe pairs at work with their brief dialogue exchange.

e. When girls are off to the side, continue working with the boys. "At the end of this unit Coyote is going to howl as his punishment from

Thought Woman. But because we don't want to disturb other classes around us, let's practice howling softly." Assess the work; reinforce the soft howling needed and continue. "Coyotes, now that you've got the pouch begin moving around the space as if you're traveling to the south. As you continue you become more tired and more hungry. Stop and rest. Look at the pouch and begin to wonder if there's anything in it to eat. But show through your face that you're thinking whether it would be a smart thing to open it up or not. You've made a decision; take the pouch and open it and see what happens." If lights were dimmed, a special moment can be created if the leader turns the lights on or creates a sound effect with a bell instrument at this point. "Thought Women, Coyote has accidentally released the stars. Come to your partners, tell them what their fate will be and leave Coyote." After the scene has been played, ask players to drop their roles and come together in a circle.

f. Assess the work of the players, focusing on their ability to follow directions for playing. Praise what was done effectively. Discuss the procedures for the next unit. Boys will continue as Coyote and girls will now portray Mouse as the medicine man. Boys are observing at the side while the leader works with the girls. "In your own space, shape your body as if you're portraying Mouse. Now explore the area as Mouse, looking for and collecting roots and herbs for your medicines. Think about whether these items need to be dug, picked, or pulled. Inspect what you're collecting carefully, tasting or smelling them to find out if they'll have some future use." Observe and assess. "Keeping the same partners as before, Coyotes will enter the action and go to the Mice asking for help with their toothaches. Listen to and exchange dialogue with each other. When Coyote is cured, thank Mouse. Go." Observe the pair playing and reassemble the group when they have completed their work.

4. **ASSESS the dramatization:**
   a. Ask players to share a specific line of dialogue that was spoken during pair playings.

   b. Share with players how effectively they were able to follow directions and how they were able to create the physicality of the characters.

   c. Discuss the children's ability to interact with classmates of a different gender.

   d. If interest is high, replay the story, allowing children to select the roles they each would like to portray.

Social Studies Follow-Up

1. This story is from the Isleta. Locate on a map where the Isleta live.

2. Discuss why the character of Coyote appears in stories from different Indian tribes and nations across the country.

3. Mouse, as a medicine man, uses roots and herbs to help Coyote's pain. Discuss how plants or other things found in nature can be used to help humans with pain or illness.

4. Discuss the role of the medicine man in Native American culture. Explore if women fulfill any of the functions associated with this role.

5. A variant of this Isleta story is also found among the Dine (Navajo) nation. Discuss how and why the story found its way from one tribe to another.

Language Arts/Literature Follow-Up

1. Read other Native American stories that feature the character of Coyote. Dramatize those stories that lend themselves to improvisation.

2. Write or tell an original story featuring Mouse, as a medicine man, helping other animals or humans with their illness or pain. Dramatize the original stories in class.

3. Read other "why" or "how" stories from Native American culture. Discuss why all cultures have developed these tales to explain why or how things came to be. Dramatize those stories that lend themselves to improvisation.

"GRANDMOTHER SPIDER STEALS THE SUN"

This Cherokee legend, from a tale reported by James Mooney in the 1890s, is rich with "why" and "how" stories: how the sun and fire came to the Cherokee, why the possum's tail and the buzzard's head are bald, and how the art of pottery making was taught.

The session design, tailored for grades 3–5, utilizes powwow dance and movement as methods of dramatizing the story. No verbal improvisation is required but dialogue or narration can be incorporated, if desired.

In the beginning there was only blackness, and nobody could see anything. People kept bumping into each other and groping blindly. They said: "What this world needs is light."

Fox said he knew some people on the other side of the world who had plenty of light, but they were too greedy to share it with others. Possum said he would be glad to steal a little of it. "I have a bushy tail," he said. "I can hide the light inside all that fur." Then he set out for the other side of the world. There he found the sun hanging in a tree and lighting everything up. He sneaked over to the sun, picked out a tiny piece of light, and stuffed it into his tail. But the light was hot and burned all the fur off. The people discovered his theft and took back the light, and ever since, Possum's tail has been bald.

"Let me try," said Buzzard. "I know better than to hide a piece of stolen light in my tail. I'll put it on my head." He flew to the other side of the world and, diving straight into the sun, seized it in his claws. He put it on his head, but it burned his head feathers off. The people grabbed the sun away from him, and ever since that time Buzzard's head has remained bald.

Then Grandmother Spider said, "Let me try!" First she made a thick-walled pot out of clay. Next she spun a web reaching all the way to the other side of the world. She was so small that none of the people there noticed her coming. Quickly Grandmother Spider snatched up the sun, put it in the bowl of clay, and scrambled back home along one of the strands of her web. Now her side of the world had light, and everyone rejoiced.

Spider Woman brought not only the sun to the Cherokee, but fire with it. And besides that, she taught the Cherokee people the art of pottery making.

Session Design for "Grandmother Spider Steals the Sun"

Materials

- pieces of Native American pottery (preferably Cherokee)
- cassette tape of American Indian powwow music
- cassette tape player
- videotape of Native American powwow dance, VCR, monitor

Story Drama Activities

1. MOTIVATE children by doing one or more of the following:

   a. Show pottery pieces and ask players or discuss how pottery is made.

   b. Turn lights off in the room and ask players what life on earth would be like without the sun.

   c. Have students watch Native American dances on videotape. Discuss how dances grow out of the stories in some Native American cultures.

2. PRESENT the story: A straightforward retelling of the legend is suitable for this particular session design.

3. DRAMATIZE the story: (The dance movements described below were performed at a powwow I attended in Chinle, Arizona.)

   a. Children are assembled in a large circle. The leader recounts this description of an opening dance at a powwow: "Drums were beaten in a steady rhythm while a group of men sang. All the dancers, men and women, adults and teenagers, stood in a large circle. The leader of a tribe, who represented his people, started moving inside the circle along the dancers. He shook hands with each person whom he passed. As soon as a person shook his hand, the dancer would get behind the leader to form a line that arced around the circle of people. This continued until he had shaken hands with everyone standing inside the circle. There was a sense of respect as hands were shaken; some nodded their heads slightly to acknowledge the leader. Everyone moved forward to the beat of the drum, two steps with one foot, then two steps with the other, back and forth throughout the dance. When another circle had been completely formed everyone broke out of the circle formation and into their own area in the middle. Some people extended their arms as if to simulate flight. They still moved in the two-step pattern but each person began to rotate slowly—those with their arms extended looked as if they were flying gently through the sky. An announcer called out over a loudspeaker, 'Ay-hah! Lookin' *good, dan*cers!' These movements continued until the drums stopped beating."

   b. The leader portrays the leader of the dance described above and walks children through the movements and patterns described. After the dance has been explained and practiced in units, each component is put together for the entire opening ceremony. Powwow music played throughout will enhance the work. A cue for all to complete the dance at the end may be the leader calling out, "Ay-hah! Lookin' *good, dan*cers!"

c. Explain to players that the dramatization of the story will use movement rather than dialogue. Also explain that the way the story will be dramatized is not a replication of the way Native Americans may do it. The main objective is to explore how improvised dance and movement can be used to tell a story, much like American Indian dances that are rooted in stories and legends.

d. Without music, have players find their own space in the area. Ask them to simulate moving and groping in the dark, squinting rather than closing eyes completely so that children do not run into each other. Ask players how their movements might change with music and become more symbolic, abstract, or dancelike. With music, ask players to simulate moving in darkness but to incorporate stylized movement. Observe and assess.

e. Divide players into five small groups and assign each group to take one of the following roles: Sun, Fox, Possum, Buzzard, and Grandmother Spider. Members in each small group collaborate to create a group dance that represents their character:
   1. Members of the Sun group create an active sun that can move across the space, when needed.

   2. Members of the Fox group create a dance that has movement qualities of their character and indicates the sun's existence on the other side of the world.

   3. Members of the Possum group create a dance that shows off their bushy tail, portrays them going to the sun, placing it in their tail, and having their bushy tail burned off.

   4. Members of the Buzzard group create a dance that shows them flying to the sun, placing it on their head, and having their head feathers burned off.

   5. Members of the Spider group create a dance that shows them making a clay pot, weaving a web to the other side of the world, stealing the sun, and returning from the other side of the world.

Small groups practice for approximately five to ten minutes, then share their work with the other groups in the class. Music played throughout the practice and sharing time will help children with the spirit of the piece. The leader and groups offer responses to what they found effective plus any suggestions for more effective work, if needed. The leader can work with each group while the others in class observe.

f. Organize the small groups around the space and combine the units together so each group is aware of its entrance into the action. Begin by walking students through the sequence of actions suggested by the story. Have the Sun begin its dance in the center, then move to one side of the room, still in role as the Sun; bring the Fox into the action and have the group indicate the Sun's existence; next, have the Possum enter and move toward the group portraying the Sun; practice how the two small groups interact when the Sun is being stolen by the Possum; do the same for the Buzzard. Then bring Grandmother Spider into the action and have the Sun brought to the center of the space. The remaining groups (Fox, Possum, and Buzzard) enter as the people, once groping in darkness and now celebrating the light. Facilitate the movements that might be created at this portion of the dramatization. Ask players to provide a way of bringing closure to the dance. (In actual sessions, some have suggested I call out "Ay-hah! Lookin' *good, dan*cers!" as the cue for players to stop dancing and create a frozen tableau or picture of all groups around the Sun.)

g. Combine all units developed thus far into a "nonstop" storytelling dance with music playing throughout. Begin with the opening pow-wow dance (**a–b**), which turns into the people groping in darkness when the leader calls out, "Ay-hah!" (**d**) At a predetermined point, the players move into their small groups with the Sun in the center. The dance proceeds as practiced above (**e–f**) to its end.

4. ASSESS the dramatization:

a. The leader offers observations on the players' work. Focus can be placed on the students' ability to follow the sequence of actions for the dramatization, and on the players' movement qualities.

b. Ask players to discuss their own comfort with dramatizing this story nonverbally. Discuss how the dramatization could incorporate narration or dialogue if it were to be replayed. Discuss how this informal dramatization could be developed into a more formal product for sharing with another class.

c. Discuss the purposes of dance in Native American culture. Ask what forms of dance exist in other cultures today.

d. As time and interest allow, replay the dramatization with each small group portraying a different character.

Social Studies Follow-Up

1. Discuss the pottery-making techniques of a Native American culture in your region. Examine the design motifs on the pottery and other crafts. Discuss the symbolic significance of the motifs.

2. Discuss why a spider would be a prominent character in some Native American legends. Speculate why the spider (Anansi) also became prominent in African folklore. Discuss whether there are any connections between the two.

3. Locate regions in the United States where the Cherokee currently live. Discuss nineteenth-century history of the Cherokee to examine the reason for their spread across several states in the country.

Language Arts/Literature Follow-Up

1. Read stories from the works of Richard Erdoes and/or Paul Goble, such as *The Sound of Flutes and Other Indian Legends* (New York: Pantheon, 1976), a collaborative project that includes legends retold by Native American storytellers. Dramatize those legends that lend themselves to improvisation.

2. Read stories from other cultures that tell of the sun's origin. Compare those versions to the Cherokee legend to discover similarities and differences between the characters and their actions. Dramatize these origin stories in class.

3. Read stories from other cultures that describe why animals have certain characteristics (e.g., why Buzzard's head is bald, why Possum's tail is no longer bushy). Discuss why people created "why" stories for animals. Dramatize those stories that lend themselves to improvisation.

"HOW MOSQUITOES CAME TO BE"

This Tlingit legend (retold from an English source in 1883) is appropriate for dramatization by children in grades 3–5. It is a violent tale to some people but children seem to express delight with the contents.

The teacher plays in role as the giant. Several actions and events in the story for enactment pose creative challenges to the group.

Long ago there was a giant who loved to kill humans, eat their flesh, and drink their blood. He was especially fond of human hearts. "Unless we can get rid of this giant," people said, "none of us will be left," and they called a council to discuss ways and means.

One man said, "I think I know how to kill the monster," and he went to the place where the giant had last been seen. There he lay down and pretended to be dead.

Soon the giant came along. Seeing the man lying there, he said: "These humans are making it easy for me. Now I don't even have to catch and kill them; they die right on my trail, probably from fear of me!"

The giant touched the body. "Ah, good," he said, "this one is still warm and fresh. What a tasty meal he'll make; I can't wait to roast his heart."

The giant flung the man over his shoulder, and the man let his head hang down as if he were dead. Carrying the man home, the giant dropped him in the middle of the floor right near the fireplace. Then he saw that there was no firewood and went to get some.

As soon as the monster had left, the man got up and grabbed the giant's huge skinning knife. Just then the giant's son came in, bending low to enter. He was still small as giants go, and the man held the big knife to his throat. "Quick, tell me, where's your father's heart? Tell me or I'll slit your throat!"

The giant's son was scared. He said: "My father's heart is in his left heel."

Just then the giant's left foot appeared in the entrance, and the man swiftly plunged the knife into the heel. The monster screamed and fell down dead.

Yet the giant still spoke. "Though I'm dead, though you killed me, I'm going to keep on eating you and all the other humans in the world forever!"

"That's what you think!" said the man. "I'm about to make sure that you never eat anyone again." He cut the giant's body into pieces and burned each one in the fire. Then he took the ashes and threw them into the air for the winds to scatter.

Instantly each of the particles turned into a mosquito. The cloud of ashes became a cloud of mosquitoes, and from their midst the man heard the giant's voice laughing, saying: "Yes, I'll eat you people until the end of time."

And as the monster spoke, the man felt a sting, and a mosquito started sucking his blood, and then many mosquitoes stung him, and he began to scratch himself.

Session Design for "How Mosquitoes Came to Be"

Story Drama Activities

1. MOTIVATE children by doing one or more of the following:

    a. Ask players what giants are and what threats they pose to humans.

    b. Discuss the nature of the mosquito and the irritant it can be to people.

    c. Discuss why mosquitoes exist. After discussion, segue into the legend.

2. PRESENT the story: The story is shared in units as the dramatization progresses. For the first unit, the leader introduces students to the conflict of the legend by retelling only the first paragraph of "How Mosquitoes Came to Be."

3. DRAMATIZE the story:

    a. Assemble the children as members of the tribe and discuss ideas for getting rid of the giant. The teacher plays in role as leader of the meeting and facilitates the discussion. As ideas are generated the leader can counter suggestions with additional points to consider ("Yes, we can do that, but it would take a very long time and too many people would get killed," or "That might work, but the giant could very easily discover what we're planning—he's very clever."). The purpose is not to negate children's suggestions but to get them to consider alternatives and possible problems that may occur with their initial ideas. Other questions might ask children to share what things have happened to them or their families as a result of the giant's destruction.

    b. The teacher steps out of role and offers feedback on the players' ideas. Point out ideas that may have been appropriate to the setting of the culture. The leader then continues with the story from the point where the man's idea of playing dead is introduced, and stops after the giant leaves to get more firewood.

    c. The leader might ask if players have suggestions for dramatizing this second unit. Most often, children elect to have the leader play the giant and one child play the man playing dead. (If players reach consensus on a different suggestion and the leader feels comfortable facilitating the dramatization as children envision it, then pursue the idea that captures the players' interest most.) If the leader is selected as the giant and one child (boy or girl) as the man who plays dead, ask players how the teacher, as giant, might simulate carrying the man across his shoulder. Though some might suggest the leader actually lift and carry the child, the leader could share he may not have the strength or he would feel uncomfortable doing so. When an acceptable solution is negotiated, practice it before continuing.

d. For the playing of the unit, explain that students will return back into role as the tribe at their meeting. The child who plays dead will share that idea with the rest of the members. The leader, in role as the giant, will make his entrance. Members of the tribe will scatter to hide (advise players not to scream as the giant approaches, but to move swiftly and silently away). The giant will then "lift and carry" the dead man to the area designated as the giant's home. After the scenario has been discussed, dramatize the unit.

e. The leader reassembles the class and retells the remaining portion of the story. (Again, player suggestions for dramatizing the unit can be solicited and facilitated by the leader if different from the following description.) Most often, children elect to have another child (boy or girl) play the giant's son. Discuss how the action of holding the imaginary knife against the son's throat and plunging it into the giant's heel can be done safely and comfortably. Practice the physical actions. Ask players to offer dramatization suggestions for how the giant's body can be cut into pieces, burned, scattered, and turned into mosquitoes. (Student ideas from actual sessions have been: the giant "pretends" to be cut into pieces and burned as all players turn into buzzing mosquitoes when the ashes are scattered; or, all players simulate being stung by mosquitoes when the giant's ashes are scattered.) Once decisions have been reached by the class, and all physical actions have been practiced, dramatize the final unit of the story.

4. ASSESS the dramatization:
   a. Ask players how easy or difficult it was to create solutions for dramatizing the unique actions of this story. Ask if different ways of portraying the actions and the giant himself can be done if the story were to be replayed.

   b. Offer feedback to children on the way physical safety was maintained and respected when the story was dramatized.

   c. Discuss why giants exist as characters in stories from different cultures. Ask players what might be implied when average-sized humans can conquer giants.

   d. If player interest remains high, dramatize all units of the story from beginning to end. Select different children to portray the man who plays dead, the giant's son, and the giant.

Social Studies Follow-Up

1. Locate on a map of the North American continent where the Tlingit live.

2. A variant of this story is in the canon of legends from the Yakima. Examine the geographical distance between the Tlingit and Yakima, and discuss why and how this same legend came to exist in the two tribes' canons.

3. Read the Greek myth of Achilles. Discuss why and how the motif of a vulnerable heel would appear in a story from two distinctively different and geographically distant cultures. Dramatize the Greek myth in class.

Language Arts/Literature Follow-Up

1. Discuss the similarities and differences between the giants and their actions in "How Mosquitoes Came to Be" and a traditional retelling of "Jack and the Beanstalk."

2. Locate and read other stories from different Native American cultures that explain how or why things came to be. Dramatize those stories that lend themselves to improvisation.

3. Read Verna Aardema's *Why Mosquitoes Buzz in People's Ears* (New York: Dial Press, 1975). Discuss the similarities and differences between these "how" and "why" stories. Discuss how and why a small mosquito would be important enough to be included in a culture's story canon. Dramatize Aardema's retelling of the African story.

"THE WARNING"

This haunting story foretells the arrival of Spanish explorers on the western American continent. It is only one of many stories that describe the White settlers arriving in this country. The story ends abruptly and does not go into the violent history that followed.

The session design is tailored for children in grades 4–6 with some experience in verbal improvisation. Unlike other session designs, this one is not as structured since it relies on decisions by the group and leader to direct the action. The story is intended as a springboard for examining the thoughts and feelings of these Pueblo villagers as they faced a moment that would change their lives forever.

When I was a little boy, my grandfather told me that a long time before the white people came to this country, there were no other villages near the pueblo of Old Laguna. There was no way to travel but by walking on trails that wound along the sides of mountains and forests.

Those were dangerous days, because our Indians warred with many other tribes. They fought with bows and arrows. Old men made strong bows and sharp arrows. The young men used them in the hunt and in war.

There were tribes who sometimes came and carried away the food, grain, pottery, and other belongings of the people. The young men of the village would be away at war for many days. Often they would return with captives. Sometimes the young men never returned.

There were many caves under the Laguna village. One of these caves was under the center of the plaza. To this cave the Indians went to pray and at evening often sang to the spirit who lived far below.

Often, after a time of prayer and singing above this cave, the old men would listen at a small opening. This opening led to a hollow place under the earth. The men often received messages there. A voice would tell them what was going to happen.

One night, old Es-cha-ya listened. Everybody was quiet for a long time. At last the old man sat up.

"I hear strange things tonight," he said. "I hear men talking. Their shoes are hard. I hear their steps. They call to others. They laugh. They carry strange knives, hard and sharp, but not of stone. Their faces, white and hairy, are not those of our people. They will come among us. They will live in our country. They have things to harm us, but we can keep their harm away. Do not wear their hard shoes that make noise with every step, or our young men will never run again. Do not eat their soft food. If anyone should, his teeth will fall from his mouth."

At this time, the people went away to their homes for the night. The old ones continued to listen at the cave. When morning came, all the young men were called from their beds. They were told to make a sacred dancing place over the cave and cover it from sight. The young men did as they were told.

It was not long before the Spaniards came, wearing beards and hard shoes. They never knew how the village of Laguna had been warned of their coming.

Session Design for "The Warning"

Materials

- cassette tape player
- Native American music (preferably of the Pueblo)

Story Drama Activities

1. MOTIVATE children by doing one or more of the following:

a. Ask students what a prophecy is and how one might be given.

b. Ask students "What would you and your family do and how would you feel if you were told you had to leave your home tomorrow because someone else was forcing you out and moving into your house?"

c. Ask students what they know of the clashes between White invaders and Native American tribes in early United States history.

d. The leader, in role as Es-cha-ya, tells the class there is danger approaching their village. The leader tells children the warning given to him from the cave spirit. (If this motivation strategy is used, proceed directly to **b** under "DRAMATIZE the story.")

2. PRESENT the story:
Depending on the approach the leader takes with the session, telling the story may not be essential if the children are thrust immediately into the playing by the leader as Es-cha-ya. If the story is to be dramatized in a conventional manner, the leader may wish to stop the story immediately after the prophecy is revealed to allow students to speculate on the outcome.

3. DRAMATIZE the story:

a. Establishing a sense of community and equipping students with knowledge about the tribe's way of life would be helpful for the playing. Discuss daily existence in the lives of the Pueblo Indians from the past and specific tasks mentioned or implied in the story (e.g., constructing bows and arrows, making pottery, farming, hunting, taking care of those wounded in wars). Ask students to share specific daily tasks of the people to generate more ideas for playing. Depending on the leader's need to maintain a sense of historical accuracy, some tasks may be designated as gender-specific. The primary goal of the session, however, is not to learn about gender roles in early Pueblo life, but to focus on the universal concerns of the people within the culture during this time period. With music playing softly, ask each child to choose a particular task to undertake. "Finding your own space and working silently, begin pantomiming the task you've selected as part of your daily routine." Observe and sidecoach in role: "That's a fine bow you've made; it will be good for the next battle." "Plant the seed deeply or it may not grow." Stepping out of role, tell the group to continue their work, but "show through your actions, your face, your body, that something is wrong. Things don't feel right, and there's a strange sense inside you that something bad is about to happen." Observe the work, then call the tribe together.

b. The leader, in role, facilitates a tribal village meeting with all players to discuss the warning he received from the cave spirit. Through strategic questions and improvised dialogue to children's responses, focus on the implications the prophecy has for the tribe's way of life and their future. The primary goal is to get students to debate and think carefully about actions and consequences rather than to make hasty decisions: "When the strangers come, what shall we do?" "Should we greet them peacefully, fight, or leave our home before they arrive?" "What danger might we face?" "If we leave, where do we go?" As a player responds, affirm or counter the suggestion or idea with supportive commentary or additional ideas for reflection: "But if we fight, how can we protect ourselves from their long, sharp knives?" "Not all of us may be willing to sacrifice our lives for that." "We've already lost many of our finest men and women in the wars." "Yes, that would be a way to keep the children safe."

c. The leader, in role as Es-cha-ya, persuades the people to spend the night reflecting on the choices put forth by the villagers and to wait by the cave for advice. Dropping out of role, the leader asks children what insights or discoveries may have been made about the Indians confronting this problem and themes that may have been generated from the village meeting. Discuss the "fight-or-flight" nature of people, and how the possibilities for action by the Pueblo may be more complex than simply fighting or leaving.

d. Discuss the importance of the cave and cave spirit to these people. Ask students to select a designated area in the room as the opening to the underground cave. Discuss how the Pueblos may have paid homage to the cave (based on what the story shares and what anthropology records). Working as facilitator, assist the class with developing a ceremony that honors the cave spirit through physical actions, dance, chanting, or singing. Again, the leader decides if the need for historical accuracy merits the selection of culturally-specific rituals, but the primary goal of this unit is to focus on the belief system of the people. This open-ended unit is preparatory work to the closure of the session. Depending on the class, small-group work might be more time-efficient. If possible, dim the lights in the room. Groups of four to five students are given approximately ten minutes to develop a brief ceremony from their "family" that honors and evokes the cave spirit. Groups may be given a theme for their work, such as "Homage from the Pottery Makers," or "Honor from the Bow and Arrow Makers." Before each group shares their ceremony, the leader facilitates a whole-village ceremony that will bring each villager together around the cave opening, and informs the players ahead of time that after the final ceremony he will become Es-cha-ya and provide the final set of instructions. Encourage the group to be as silent as possible during the final moments. One group at a time then shares its prepared ceremony, finishing with the entire village ceremony.

e. Immediately after the village ceremony, the leader drops into role as Es-cha-ya and says, "Spirit of the cave, your people are listening. We will sit and try to hear your words. We will sit and open our hearts to what *you* would have us do and not what *we* want to do. We will wait patiently and listen in silence. You have given us a warning, but tell us what we are now to do." Allow for one minute of silence. If a student begins to speak, motion for quiet or ask for silence in role.

4. ASSESS the dramatization:

a. When the leader determines that the group has reached its maximum tolerance for listening, he drops out of role and tells students to relax. Ask if they were able to concentrate on listening to the cave spirit and what they believed it told the people of the village to do. Discuss why the Pueblo Indians in this village placed so much importance on the cave spirit for guidance.

b. Ask players what feelings the people might have experienced when they first heard the warning and dealt with the approaching danger.

c. Discuss recent or current events that involve countries at war over invasions or land disputes. Ask students to compare the plight of the Pueblos described in the story with contemporary political situations, noting the similarities.

d. If the ending of the story was withheld from players, share how Grammer concludes "The Warning." Ask players what choice they think the people in this story made and what history records.

Social Studies Follow-Up

1. Locate on a map where the Pueblo Indians lived before the arrival of Spanish colonists.

2. Discuss why certain Indian tribes were at war with each other.

3. Report on particular historical accounts of Native American tribes who confronted White settlers new to the continent. Focus on incidents of tribes forced to relocate as the United States territory expanded. Use improvisation to dramatize these encounters between the U.S. government and selected Indian nations.

4. Select a particular Native American tribe in your region and discuss its spiritual beliefs and practices.

5. Examine and discuss contemporary news accounts of Indian tribes and nations in dispute with federal and state governments. Compare how the disputes are handled today and how they were handled during various periods of history.

Language Arts/Literature Follow-Up

1. The spirit in the cave provided a warning to the tribe. Write a prophecy poem to the American people of today.

2. Write an imaginary account of a White settler seeing a Native American Indian for the very first time. Then write an account of a Native American Indian seeing a White settler for the very first time. Focus on physical descriptions of the people and the first impressions, feelings, and fears one might have about seeing the other. Compare the two points of view. Improvise various ways two people from different cultures may react toward each other when meeting for the first time.

3. Read Scott O'Dell's *Sing Down the Moon* (Boston: Houghton Mifflin Co., 1970). The action of this novel is set centuries later than the first encounter depicted in "The Warning." Discuss to what degree O'Dell's depiction of the Indian characters, their dialogue, and their actions may be culturally sensitive or offensive to contemporary Native Americans. Discuss what is needed by a non-Indian writer who wants to develop a culturally sensitive work about Native American people. Find selections from the novel that lend themselves to dramatization and improvise the scenes in class.

5

Stories from the Asian and Pacific Islands Canons

"THE FIRST MONKEYS"

The story below is retold rather melodramatically, with several vocabulary words beyond the comprehension of most young children. It is reproduced as originally published, and teachers are advised to retell this story in their own words. "The First Monkeys" has an intriguing and very playable story line. Grades K–4 can dramatize the folktale, and children from the upper grade levels may develop more in-depth characterizations for the nobility. The accompanying session design is tailored for children new to drama.

Long, long ago, King Ramos ruled over the island kingdom of Basuanga. He was harsh to his subjects to the point of being cruel and a despot. His queen possessed similar traits which did not endear her to the people.

They were naturally a very rich couple. The palace in which they lived was a huge complex, filled with the most beautiful and expensive furniture in the world. As King Ramos and his spouse loved good food, their storerooms were filled with different foods and imported wines.

A confirmed gourmet, King Ramos threw grand receptions, where all manner of delicacies were served. But he and the Queen being status conscious would invite only the nobility who matched their rank as rulers.

These people, well fed and looked after by the generous hosts, became their friends. These invitees often dined and wined at the palace but they had no idea that the King was a heartless monarch who was cruel to the core and the Queen was not the lovable person that she appeared at these lavish parties.

King Ramos loved these grand receptions. One day he and his Queen were hosts of a festive party that went on for the whole day. A number of tables were laid with the richest foods and viands and the choicest wines. Since it was a whole-day affair, and the weather was good, the generous hosts had the tables removed to the palace garden. The guests had a whale of a time, eating and carousing even as the Romans used to, in hoary times. There was laughter and merriment all around.

An old decrepit woman somehow appeared on the scene. Bent with age and clad in rags she hobbled around the tables, begging for food and alms. Nobody took any notice of her. Those that did only tried to shoo her away.

Finally, the miserable hag approached the table around which the King and his cohorts were dining and wining. Folding her hands, she pleaded, "Please, Sire, give me some food. I am famished and starving!"

The Queen, sitting beside King Ramos, saw the beggar woman and became very angry. She shouted, "Who admitted you to the palace garden? Beggar woman, away with you! Don't you know this reception is for the nobility only, not for beggars like you?"

This harsh repartee somehow provided amusement to the guests around the table. They guffawed. One of them threw a spoon at the old beggar woman. Others followed suit, laughing all the while. The poor beggar woman dodged the spoons as these fell in her direction.

King Ramos was entertained by this game and exclaimed, with glee, "Keep it up, my friends! The first guests to hit the hag on the head will receive a prize."

The old woman was in a fix. She knew not what to do—the spoons hitting her all over. Nobody could come to her rescue. The cruel fun at her expense went on, the merry-makers hardly suspecting that this crass apathy would cost them dearly.

The scene changed all of a sudden. Before the very eyes of the King Ramos and his merry-making guests, the old woman disappeared, vanishing into thin air, as a shaft of blinding white light struck her. The revellers, amazed at this phenomenon, saw that in the same instant, she was replaced by a beautiful woman, dressed from head to toe in shimmering white. A halo surrounded her lovely face but it shone with such a glare that the beholders could barely look at her.

The lady in white had not appeared on the troubled spot for nothing. She had a mission to fulfill. In righteous anger, she addressed the assembled guests, "King Ramos and guests, you are despicable, cruel-hearted people, indeed, the scum of the earth. None among you has a kind heart or any feeling of compassion. You have been born as privileged people but you don't deserve to be humans. Hence, you—all of you—will be transformed into animals. But, it is decreed, that you will be special animals—the ones that resemble humans and can also behave like men."

The lady having pronounced these words, a more strange phenomenon took place. The selfsame spoons that had been wildly thrown at the beggar woman, rose up, flew like darts and hit King Ramos, the Queen and their guests on their buttocks with such force that they cried in pain.

This was not the end of the dire punishment. The clothes of the men and the dresses of the ladies changed to long hair covering their bodies. Their hands grew longer and were also covered with hair—the fineries having vanished in a trice. Instead of walking on two legs, they ambled around, and the only sound they could emit in their new state was "Kur . . . kurr . . . kurrraa."

Looking at each other, and realizing how ugly they had become, they ran in a body to the nearby forest, where their companions were wild pigs and deer. They and their progeny lived there ever since. These were the first monkeys in the Philippines.

Session Design for "The First Monkeys"

Materials

- illustration of a monkey
- illustrations of the affluent/nobility and the poor

Story Drama Activities

1. MOTIVATE children by doing one or more of the following:
   a. Show an illustration of a monkey and discuss its characteristics. Discuss how the animal is similar to and different from a human being.

   b. Show illustrations of the affluent and poor. Aside from wealth, discuss the differences between being rich and poor. Ask students how the everyday lives of people with different incomes and statuses separate them socially.

   c. Discuss the possible consequences of those who treat others cruelly or mockingly.

2. PRESENT the story: Retell Mariano's story with a more age-appropriate vocabulary.

3. DRAMATIZE the story: Selected units from the story are practiced first, since player interest in them may be high.

a. Ask players to find their own space in the room. Practice the transformation from a person of nobility into a monkey. "First, create a posture that suggests you're a king, queen, or other member of royalty. Without any sounds and without disturbing anyone else in the room, shape your body to create a monkey." Observe and assess. "Come back to human form as a member of royalty. Let me count from one to five. As I count, slowly change your body from the human form to the monkey shape without any sounds." Slowly count from one to five and observe the players' work. "Now let's see what happens when you softly change your voice from human speech and language to monkey sounds as you're changing your physical shape from royalty to the animal. What are some things these people might be saying to themselves or to each other at this point in the story?" Solicit ideas from players and encourage them to select or improvise with the suggestions offered. Lead children through the complete transformation from human posture and language into animal shapes and sounds. Have all players gather together and assess the work.

b. Discuss the attitudes of the nobility toward the poor as illustrated in the story. Ask players to describe the feelings and reactions the royalty might have upon seeing a poor person. Ask players how the poor would feel and react to the nobility's reaction. Divide the class into split-half groups; half will portray the nobility while the other half will portray the poor. Those who are members of royalty are asked to stand on one side of the room while the half playing the poor are on the other side. Sidecoach to the nobility that they are to imagine getting dressed for the King and Queen's reception: "Put on your finest robes, hats, jewelry, and shoes and think about the fine banquet you'll be attending. First, think how a member of the nobility would walk across the space. Show through your face, body, and movement how your character might proceed to the banquet. Go." Observe and assess. Ask players portraying the poor to find their own space on the floor in the center of the room: "Position and shape your body as you think someone who's very poor might sit. Without any sounds, try to show they're hungry, tired, and that life is very hard for them. Begin." Observe, sidecoach as needed, and assess the players' work. Ask players portraying the poor to move to one side of the room and remain seated as if they were alongside a road. Ask players portraying the nobility to walk across the space and demonstrate a possible reaction to the poor people by the side of the road. Reinforce that no physical contact is to be made between the groups. Children in upper grade levels might improvise comments or dialogue with each other during this unit (e.g., begging for money, comments on the smell of the poor, etc.). Allow verbal work as long as players' remarks are appropriate to the characters. As time allows, ask each split-half group to reverse roles and play through the same actions described above. Assess the work and discuss the reactions and remarks that may have emerged from the playing.

c. Discuss what members of the nobility would eat at King Ramos' reception (e.g., fresh fruit, fish, special dishes of the country) and what topics of conversation would be raised (e.g., the food, their land, wealth, servants, each other's clothing, jewelry). The leader informs players he will play in role as King Ramos and speak with children as if they were at the reception. Ask players to pantomime eating some of they food items mentioned above. Utilize the topics children mentioned and use closed- and open-ended questioning to solicit language from children: "That's a beautiful robe. Is it new?" "Look at all that jewelry. Are those diamonds you're wearing?" "What shall we do with all the poor people in the kingdom? They are such a nuisance." Improvise with children and assist them with their verbal characterizations of nobility.

d. The leader selects two children to portray the King and Queen. The leader plays the role of the Old Woman. Discuss what dialogue might occur between the Old Woman and the Queen (as outlined in the story), and the initiating line of dialogue from the King for the guests to throw things at the Old Woman. Ask players to suggest some sort of gesture or action the leader can do to show he has changed into the woman surrounded by the halo, and a gesture that begins the transformation of the nobility into monkeys. Finally, discuss how the playing will come to an end once the transformation has been completed (e.g., the monkeys freeze in place; the monkeys move to one side of the room and huddle together). Once these decisions have been made and reviewed, the unit is played.

e. Reinforce to children that during the final unit of playing, no physical contact is to be made with the leader, and no things are to be actually thrown. The leader steps out of the circle, announces he is in role, and begins begging the nobility for food. Improvise with children as they initiate dialogue and solicit oral responses from the guests. Approach the Queen and King and dialogue according to the decisions made above. Improvise the final decree by the woman with the halo and make the gesture or action that transforms the humans into monkeys.

4. ASSESS the dramatization:

a. Assess the final unit of the dramatization, focusing on the players' ability to follow directions and adhere to the decisions made by the group.

b. Discuss how movement and language or sound were used to create the characters in the story. Ask players to describe why some physical and verbal choices are more appropriate than others when creating characters from a story.

c. Discuss how the tale is not only a story of how monkeys came to be, but also a warning to those who are cruel to others. Discuss why the wealthy rather than the poor were selected for those who were changed into monkeys.

d. If time permits, replay the final unit of the story with different children recast as the King and Queen and a child as the Old Woman.

Social Studies Follow-Up

1. Locate the Philippines on a globe or map.

2. Discuss the language(s) spoken in the Philippines by the majority of its citizens today.

3. Discuss the Spanish colonization of the Philippines. Examine what influences the European and Asian cultures had on this country.

4. With older groups, discuss the overthrow of the Philippine government under Ferdinand Marcos. In what ways does "The First Monkeys" parallel the historic event?

5. Discuss how wealth and poverty affect human relationships and relationships between countries.

Language Arts/Literature Follow-Up

1. Read "The First Monkeys" from Victor Montejo's *The Bird Who Cleans the World and Other Mayan Fables* (Willimantic, CT: Curbstone Press, 1991). Compare Mariano's story from the Philippines with Montejo's version from Guatemala. Describe how the origin of monkeys is similar in these two stories, and discuss why such similarities might be present in stories from these two countries. Dramatize Montejo's version of the story in class.

2. Read tales from other Asian and Pacific Island cultures that feature a monkey as a central character. Describe why a monkey might be portrayed as a lowly character in some stories, and a loveable yet

powerful character in others. Dramatize stories that lend themselves to improvisation.

3. Find the definitions for some of the following vocabulary words used in Mariano's story (arranged in the order they appear in the tale): despot, endear, complex, imported, confirmed, gourmet, receptions, delicacies, status, conscious, invitees, monarch, lavish, viands, carousing, hoary, decrepit, alms, cohorts, famished, repartee, guffawed, crass, apathy, revellers, phenomenon, righteous, despicable, compassion, privileged, decreed, selfsame, dire, ambled, progeny. Replay "The First Monkeys" or develop original improvisations in which several of these vocabulary words are integrated into the dialogue.

4. Discuss how oral language use and vocabulary for people with higher incomes might be different from those with lower incomes. Discuss what social conditions might influence the way we speak.

"THE RAVEN AND THE STAR FRUIT TREE"

Nikki Hu, a Chinese American dancer whose work with children has been explored through interactive television, introduced me to this story at one of her workshops. She learned the story from Vietnamese children in Boston and adopted it as one of the stories used in her residencies. Lê Phạm Thúy-kim, an instructor at Arizona State University, reviewed this version and shared that it is one of the most well-known folk tales from Vietnam, yet different versions exist with varying motifs. In some retellings the bird is a hawk or the mythical phoenix. Handmade sacks [three-by-three for the younger brother and nine-by-nine for the eldest brother] are used instead of the basket and trunk described in the adaptation below. In spite of the differing motifs there is no "standard" version of this story, according to Lê.

This tale is not only about sibling rivalry, it is also about the rewards for kindness and the punishment for greed. Children in grades 2–4 will grasp the apparent moral of the story, but older grade levels may also find more complexities in the motivations behind the brothers' actions.

A father had two sons whom he loved very much. The older son was rough and cruel to his little brother, but the younger son was gentle and kind to everyone—even to his older brother.

Before the father died he divided his fortune into two portions— one for each of his sons. To the oldest child he gave all his money and jewelry. To the youngest child he gave a star fruit tree. The older brother rejoiced at his new wealth. The younger brother felt troubled by his own simple gift but accepted it graciously from his father. As the oldest son counted his money daily the youngest son slept contentedly underneath his star fruit tree.

One day a raven flew onto one of the branches and started pecking at a piece of the sweet, ripe fruit. The young boy awoke when the raven squawked with delight. He started to shoo the bird away but then considered that the poor bird might be hungry, so he allowed the raven to eat its fill.

"Get a basket and climb on my back," the raven squawked. The little boy was amazed to hear the raven speak and thought it must be magic. "Get a basket and climb on my back," the raven squawked again. The youngest boy did as he was told. He brought a small basket and climbed on the raven's back. They then flew far, far away, over the endless sea to the top of a magic mountain made of gold where there were pieces of the precious rock in abundance. "Take what you will," the raven said.

The little boy filled his small basket with pieces of gold. When the basket could hold no more he got on the raven's back and they flew far, far, over the endless sea and back home. The youngest son threw a celebration for his friends to share his newfound wealth.

The older brother became jealous of his younger brother's wealth and demanded to know how he came upon this fortune. The little brother shared how the magic raven took him to a magic mountain of gold and allowed him to fill a basket with treasure. The older brother, rich as he was yet not satisfied with his own wealth, convinced his little brother to take the money and jewelry given to him by their father in exchange for the star fruit tree. And the little boy obliged his older brother.

The next day the oldest boy waited underneath the tree for the magic raven to return. When the bird arrived it landed on a branch and started pecking at the sweet, ripe fruit. But instead of letting the raven eat, the older brother grabbed the bird and demanded to be taken to the magic mountain of gold. "Get a basket and climb on my back," the raven squawked. But the older brother, greedy for wealth, did not bring a small basket as his brother had but a large and heavy trunk. The raven and the boy flew far, far away, over the endless sea to the magic mountain where he quickly loaded his trunk to the top with large rocks of gold. The trunk was so full he could barely close it, but somehow he managed to do it. He climbed on the raven's back and set the heavy trunk with gold next to him. The magic raven, weighted down with wealth, could barely lift itself off the ground. But the raven spread its wings and gained flight, carrying the oldest brother with his heavy trunk of gold far, far, over the endless sea.

But because the boy had been so greedy and took more gold than the bird could carry, the raven became exhausted and collapsed in midair, throwing the oldest brother and his trunk of gold far, far into the bottom of the endless sea. The boy drowned and the gold was forever buried underwater.

The raven, rid of its burden and now able to fly with ease, returned to the star fruit tree to eat its fill.

Session Design for "The Raven and the Star Fruit Tree"

Materials

- star fruit

Story Drama Activities

1. MOTIVATE children by doing one or more of the following:
   a. Ask players to describe problems that might be encountered between siblings. Depending on the grade level of the group, describe "sibling rivalry."

   b. Discuss the possible consequences of greed, or the adage, "Good things come to those who wait."

   c. Show children a piece of star fruit. Describe where it is grown primarily. Segue into the presentation of the story.

2. PRESENT the story: A straightforward presentation of the tale is all that is needed for the dramatization.

3. DRAMATIZE the story:
   a. Discuss the characterizations of the two brothers. Ask players how the older brother would respond when he heard news about his inheritance. Then ask how the younger brother would respond to news about his inheritance. Solicit what may be specific lines of dialogue spoken by the sons: "How much money will I get?" or "Thank you, Father, for your gift." The leader plays in role as the father and the children are divided into split-half groups—one half as the older and one half as the younger brother. The leader shares in role, "Because I am getting older, I've decided to divide my estate before I leave you. To my older son, I leave all my money and jewelry. And to my younger son, I leave—a star fruit tree." If players verbalize responses, improvise with them or elaborate on their responses: "What will you do with all the money I'm leaving you?" "My youngest, are you disappointed?" Assess the players' verbal work in this

unit. If interest is sustained, have each half of the class reverse their roles and replay the scene.

b. Ask all players to take on the role of the younger son while the leader plays in role as the elder. Discuss what material needs the younger son would have if he has no money. Ask players to improvise a scenario with the leader: The younger son will ask his older brother for financial or material assistance (money for a home, food, etc.); the older brother will be denying all of his requests. Ask players to generate a character-appropriate rationale for the younger son's requests or manner of asking (e.g., begging rather than demanding; gentle rather than angry). The leader can also ask such challenging questions as: "Why do you think Father gave all his money to me?" "Why should I help you? I'm the one who looked after you when you were growing up. What have you ever done for me?" After the improvisation has reached an appropriate closing point, assess the players' work at generating dialogue and their perceptions of being in a helpless situation with a family member.

c. Discuss possible ways for dramatizing the scene between the raven and the younger son. "How can we show that a raven is on a tree branch?" "How do we play out the action where the raven carries the younger son on its back in flight?" If the group generates playable ideas, the leader should feel free to incorporate them into the dramatization of the unit. If the group is at a loss for ideas, pair playing can be utilized with one partner as the raven and the other partner as the young son. Narrative pantomime can be employed by the leader once decisions have been made on how the raven will land on a tree branch and "carry" the child across the sea. Preparatory discussion on the use of space in the classroom (respecting each other's space, staying within boundaries, etc.) is essential before the playing. The leader's narration can be read directly from the story, beginning with "One day a raven flew onto one of the branches . . ." and ending with ". . . he got on the raven's back and they flew far, far, over the endless sea and back home." Assess the players' nonverbal work and their ability to develop creative solutions for dramatizing the unit's action.

d. Discuss the older son's relationship with and attitude toward his younger brother now that the wealth is somewhat equal between them. "What might the older son be thinking about, or how would he be feeling toward his younger brother now that he has the gold?" The leader plays in role as the younger son and children now take on the role of the older one. Improvise the unit in which the older brother asks about the gold and convinces his brother to give him the star fruit tree in exchange for their father's money and jewels.

e. Players continue as the older brother while the leader now plays in role as the raven. Suggest that the raven will be asking questions to try to understand the brother's needs when it lands on the star fruit tree. Also ask players how everyone working in ensemble might simulate flying on and falling from the raven's back, then drowning in the sea. Once these decisions have been discussed and played out physically, the leader enters the action as the raven eating from the star fruit tree. Questions that might be posed to the older brother as the unit progresses are "How did you learn about the gold on the magic mountain?" "Why is it so important for you to be richer?" "Why should I take you to the magic mountain?" "What are you going to do with all that gold once we return?" "I can't fly with all that weight on me. Why don't you throw some of the gold into the sea to make it easier on me?" After the unit has been dramatized, assess the players' work with particular attention to the appropriateness of their verbal responses as the older brother.

4. ASSESS the dramatization:

a. Ask players to compare and contrast the characterizations of the two brothers. "What did you find yourself doing differently to portray the older brother in the last part of the dramatization?"

b. Discuss whether goodness and generosity are always rewarded, or evil and greed always punished. "Aside from money, what other rewards exist for being good?" "Why are some people greedy? Why are money or property so important to them that they're unwilling to share what they have?"

c. This story has been dramatized by other groups through movement and dance. Ask players how the story might be replayed without dialogue. As time and interest allow, explore a nonverbal dramatization of "The Raven and the Star Fruit Tree" set to folk music from Vietnam.

d. Ask players what the star fruit tree in the story might symbolize.

Social Studies Follow-Up

1. Locate Vietnam on a globe or map.

2. Discuss why a story that features a star fruit tree would have developed in Vietnam but not in the U.S. or Europe.

3. Discuss star fruit's primary geographic region of growth, climate needs, etc.

4. A variant of Vietnam's "The Raven and the Star Fruit Tree" is found in the folk literature of China. Locate both countries on a map or globe and discuss how the story may have been transmitted from one country to another. Explore the history of China's influence on Vietnam to help develop an answer.

Language Arts/Literature Follow-Up

1. Read other Vietnamese folktales or selections from the children's folk poetry of Vietnam. Dramatize stories that lend themselves to improvisation.

2. Locate and read stories from other cultures that include rivalry between siblings (e.g., "Cinderella"). Discuss why different cultures would have this same motif in some of their stories.

3. In many folk tales, the youngest child in a family is portrayed as the one who is rewarded. Write an original story in which the problems of a child who is the oldest or in between the youngest and oldest are portrayed. Develop the story so that these children are portrayed as the ones who are rewarded. Dramatize these stories in class.

"AUNTIE TIGER"

Three graduate students from Taiwan—Sissy Lin, Ellen Shaw, and John Huang—shared variants of this story in our improvisation with youth classes at Arizona State University. We were intrigued by the classic folk figure of Auntie Tiger and began incorporating the story in our own sessions, primarily in grades 2–4.

There are many tales that include Auntie Tiger, and this version is just one of the adventures between children and the magic beast. This story is extremely violent from an American perspective, but consider that this tale comes from a different culture with different values and sensibilities. The accompanying session design does not dramatize the story as written but uses the basic conflict and characters as stimuli for small-group improvisation.

Taiwan was once filled with tigers. Some of them had the power to transform themselves into old women who called themselves "Auntie Tiger."

They would gain people's trust through their elderly kindness, then change back into their animal shape and eat their victims. Little children were their favorite food! Mothers and fathers who had to leave their children alone at home would tell them to lock the doors and windows and not let strangers inside. That's what the Widow Chang told her two daughters, Chuan and Lang. But they did not listen.

When the Widow Chang had to go to town, she asked her two daughters to look after the house, and she left them with a warning: "Don't let strangers inside, because one of them may be Auntie Tiger." But on the way to town the Widow Chang herself met a kind old woman (who was actually a tiger in disguise). They chatted and gossiped and the widow told the old woman about her two daughters she left at home. Then Auntie Tiger changed into a real tiger and ate the poor widow Chang.

The beast transformed itself back into an old woman and went to see Chuan and Lang at their house. Auntie Tiger knocked on the door and told the girls she was their aunt from town whom their mother asked to visit. Chuan remembered her mother's warning but little Lang did not. Lang unlocked the door, embraced her "aunt" and asked Auntie to spend the night with them.

Auntie Tiger slept in the same bed as the two young girls. Around midnight Chuan was awakened by a crunching noise. When she asked her Auntie about the sound the old woman replied that she was eating peanuts. Chuan asked for some, but was given a bloody finger instead! Chuan knew then and there that her poor little sister had been eaten by the woman, who must be Auntie Tiger. And that was when the woman changed back into the shape of the horrible beast.

Chuan remained calm and told the tiger she had to use the bathroom. The tiger tied a rope around Chuan's waist to keep its next meal from escaping. When Chuan was in the bathroom she untied the rope from her waist and tied it to a kettle of water. Whenever the tiger pulled the rope it heard the sound of pouring water which made the beast think that little Chuan was still using the bathroom. But Chuan had climbed out of the window and up into a tall tree where she hid.

When the tiger grew impatient it broke down the door to the bathroom and discovered that Chuan had escaped. The tiger ran out of the house to find Chuan but she was nowhere to be seen. The beast drank from a well next to the tree where Chuan was hiding and saw her reflection in the water.

The tiger demanded that Chuan come down, but she begged the tiger to grant her one last wish before she was eaten: "There is a sparrow in this tree. Let me fry this bird for my last meal. Send me up a pot of hot oil to cook it."

The tiger was so eager for little Chuan that it willingly obliged the girl. When the pot of boiling oil was sent up to Chuan she made herself some fried sparrow. Then she told the tiger to open its mouth wide so she could jump into it and be swallowed in one gulp.

The tiger opened its jaws wide beneath the tree, but instead of jumping, Chuan poured the pot of boiling oil into the tiger's mouth and the savage beast burned to death.

Chuan climbed down the tree and ran to town to live with her real aunt.

She grew up happily.

Session Design for "Auntie Tiger"

Materials

• illustrations of a tiger and an elderly woman

Story Drama Activities

1. MOTIVATE children by doing one or more of the following:
   a. Show pictures of a tiger and an elderly woman. Ask students how one might transform into the other if the tiger was magic.

   b. Ask players why it might be dangerous to let a stranger into one's house. Ask what the stranger might do or say to convince the home-owner to let him inside.

   c. Ask players to find their own space in the room and begin walking as they feel an old woman might. Depending on the grade level of the children, discourage what may be stereotyped portrayals of the elderly (hunched backs, shaky walks, etc.). Ask players to move around the space, silently and without any physical contact, as if they were tigers. Next ask them to begin walking around the space as an old woman, and when the leader counts from one to five they will continue walking but transform into a tiger's shape. Reverse the count so they can move and transform from a tiger into an old woman. Assess the work.

   d. Show a picture of Taiwan on a map. Introduce the character of Auntie Tiger as a classic folktale figure from the region (use as a segue into the presentation of the story).

2. PRESENT the story: Some elements of the story may be questionable for certain groups or ages. The leader should use his own discretion when choosing to edit selected portions or incidents of "Auntie Tiger" in the retelling.

3. DRAMATIZE the story:

    a. Ask players to describe or create the vocal quality of Auntie Tiger: "What kind of voice might a sweet, older woman have?" Then ask, "What might Auntie Tiger have said behind the door to convince Lang and Chuan to let her inside the house?"

    b. Ask players to get into groups of two or three. Have players within the group select who will be Auntie Tiger (one player) and who will be the child or children (one player as Chuan, or two players as Lang and Chuan). To reinforce the use of a barrier, have players in each group place a chair between the opposing characters to simulate talking to each other through a door. (If the group is new to drama or very young, the leader may choose to play Auntie Tiger himself while all children in the class are "behind the door." Dialogue can be exchanged between the leader and the collective class.) Give directions for the improvisation: "Now that you've selected your roles, the people playing Auntie Tiger are going to knock on the door and try to convince the child or children behind it to let her in. But let's talk about some of the guidelines for working: Auntie Tiger doesn't force her way in by breaking down the door or threatening the children. She does it by her words and voice alone. The people playing the children will have to listen very carefully to what Auntie Tiger is saying, because you'll need to have an answer to everything Auntie Tiger asks or says. Sometimes you'll be asking her questions to prove who she really is, so the Auntie Tigers will have to listen carefully, too. Since we're dramatizing the story the way it was told, the Auntie Tigers will be let inside the house. But don't do it right away—wait for my signal [to be determined by the leader] and that will be a cue to bring your dialogue to a close and let Auntie Tiger inside. And once inside, you don't attack the children but greet them warmly. Are there any questions? [answer, as needed] Let's begin." Observe pairs or small groups working simultaneously to ensure all are on task. After one minute of dialogue (longer, if children are improvising well), give the signal for the children to bring their work to a close.

    c. Gather children together and ask players who portrayed Auntie Tiger to share what they said to the children to let her in. Ask players who portrayed the children what things were said or asked before Auntie Tiger was brought inside the house. If interest is still high, ask players to reverse roles and replay the improvisation (two Auntie Tigers talking to one child is acceptable) followed by an assessment.

d. Gather players together and discuss the next unit of dramatization. "The version of the story I told you is just one of many that are told about Auntie Tiger. And we have a chance to create some of the kinds of adventures and escapes children might have faced when they dealt with this character. We're going to pretend that I'll be portraying Auntie Tiger in your home, and in small groups you're going to come up with a plan for saving yourselves and escaping from the danger. But we need to work out some guidelines first. In the story Auntie Tiger was killed, but when you come up with your plan, there shouldn't be any physical harm done to anyone, otherwise we have to stop the playing. Second, we want to work on how dialogue is used to tell the story, and if your plan is just to run around and yell to confuse Auntie Tiger, then we don't get the chance to hear how you can use words to talk your way out of a dangerous problem. So no physical contact or harm, and no running around and yelling. Use words and simple actions alone. Auntie Tiger convinced you to let her inside the house. And now you have to convince Auntie Tiger to let you outside the house. I'll be exchanging dialogue with you, and I'll let you outside only if your work is believable."

e. Ask players to get into small "family" groups of four or five. (If the class is relatively small or in a lower grade level, use groups of two to four.) Once assembled, offer the students directions for their work: "Your group will have about five minutes to talk about a plan you'll use to convince Auntie Tiger to let you outside the house. Everybody in your group needs to agree on the plan, otherwise it may not work. It might help if you decide first which room in the house your improvisation will be in, like the kitchen or the bedroom. It might be set in ancient Taiwan, or it might be set in today's time. Your group decides that. Any questions? [answer, as needed.] Start talking about your plan." The leader walks throughout the room, assisting as needed. Children may be reluctant to share their preliminary plan with the leader since he will be portraying Auntie Tiger. General questions might be asked, such as, "Will everybody be doing the same thing or is each person doing something different?" After the initial planning, bring the class together and discuss contingency plans: "You've thought of an idea to get out of the house, but what will you do if it doesn't work? What if Auntie Tiger is onto you and knows your trick? You've talked about one plan, but you'll have to have a second, backup plan, just in case the first one doesn't work. In your groups, review the first idea you've developed, but now develop a second plan, just in case something goes wrong. When I play Auntie Tiger, I may not let you out of the house on your first try. Return to your work for about five more minutes." The leader assists the groups as needed.

f. Assemble the players together and review the guidelines for the improvisation: "Remember that no physical contact or harm is allowed, and no running around or yelling. We'll have to be listening really hard to each other so we can respond to each other believably. You can leave the house only if Auntie Tiger lets you." Ask groups to volunteer for the order of improvisation presentations and list on the chalkboard. As each group comes into the playing area, ask what room of the house the scene is in, and whether it takes place in earlier times or today.

g. The leader as Auntie Tiger improvises with each small group. The criteria for allowing children to leave the house should be based on whether the leader assesses the children's work to be believable, not necessarily whether their plan is creative or amusing. If some children in the group are silent or improvising minimally, the leader can ask them questions directly rather than letting the "spokesperson" contribute the majority of the dialogue. As a character with control, the leader can structure the improvisation by negating or following the direction children set for their plans. Depending on goals, the leader can actually bring the improvisation to a close without letting the children out of the house if he assesses their work to be ineffective; but he should allow them the opportunity to try again after all groups have completed their work. After each group shares their improvisation, the leader can offer what he found effective about their ideas and why the decision was made to let them out of the house.

4. ASSESS the dramatization:

a. Ask players to share what they found effective about other groups' plans or individual work during the improvisation.

b. Discuss what is needed for verbal improvisation to work effectively (listening to others, thinking quickly, helping a partner when he is at a loss for a reply, etc.).

c. Discuss what situations may exist today in which children could find themselves in danger with an adult. Offer strategies for getting away from the danger.

Social Studies Follow-Up

1. Locate Taiwan on a globe or map. Note its relationship (area, distance) to China.

2. The story mentioned that in earlier times parents left their children at home alone to watch the house. Discuss why this practice is not usually done today. Locate news articles about parents who left children at home by themselves and the consequences that resulted.

3. Discuss why animals such as a tiger and a monkey would become classic folktale figures (Auntie Tiger and The Monkey King) in Taiwan's and China's literature, but not in Europe's or America's literature.

Language Arts/Literature Follow-Up

1. The character of Auntie Tiger is featured in a cycle of stories from Taiwan and China. Write or tell an original story that uses Auntie Tiger as the antagonist. Dramatize the stories if they lend themselves to improvisation.

2. Small-group improvisations were developed that featured children escaping from Auntie Tiger. If the grade level is proficient at writing, transform the improvisation into a written play script.

3. Read stories from other cultures that feature animal characters who can transform themselves into human shape, or who are notorious for eating people. Dramatize these tales in class if they lend themselves to improvisation.

"TARO AND THE MAGIC FISH"

Folktales do not have to be ancient in origin. A Japanese American student from Washington State, Al N., shared this story with me. He mentioned it was "made up" by him and his grandparents when he was little. The story incorporates cultural elements from Japan and motifs from other Japanese folktales. The story and its accompanying session design are appropriate for grades 3–5. Puppetry for the sea creatures can play an intriguing role in its dramatization, but the session design uses people for the underwater life.

Mie (pronounced MEE-ay), a term used in the story, derives from the

Japanese Kabuki theatre. A mie *is a stylized, carefully composed, statuelike moment of tension. After a complex sequence of movements, the Kabuki actor creates a climactic pose that is nonrealistic and suggestive, paying attention to every physical detail, including the face. Imagine a picture of a triumphant warrior after a fierce battle with his sword lifted in the air; his other arm extended outward; his legs in a tense lunge; and you have an example of a* mie.

Taro, Japan's greatest general, was separated from his army during the last great battle. Tired, hungry, and thirsty, he wandered along the shores of the ocean desperate for help. He tried to drink the salty water but spat out the bitter taste from his mouth.

Turning his attention to food, Taro scouted the water in hopes of finding a creature for survival. A golden glimmer came toward the surface and Taro readied himself to strike. When the fish came closer, Taro grabbed the creature from the water and was about to eat it when the fish cried, "Honorable Lord! Please—spare my life!"

Taro dropped the fish in amazement on the wet, sandy shore. "A talking fish?" he thought to himself as he trembled. The fish began scuttling in desperation and begged, "Great Lord! Throw me back in the water, please, and I shall repay the kindness!" Taro, afraid that a severe test of faith was in store, picked up the fish and threw it into the ocean. The creature, grateful for its life, came to the surface and said, "I thank you, great general. If you need me, call, and I shall be there for you." The fish swam deeply into the blue water and disappeared.

During this haunting episode, Taro did not see the opposing general and his army advancing toward the shore. Taro heard the sound of armor, and when he turned to look, a mighty force a hundred strong was marching, swords in hand. Taro panicked and did not know where to turn. But he remembered the promise of the creature he saved, and prayed that the fish would keep its word.

"We meet once more," said the opposing general. The army came to a halt and stared at Taro's exhausted body. "Are you ready to die?" Taro raised his arms and announced to the soldiers, "Fools! You think a hundred men can stop the mighty Taro? The power I have is so great it can even command the creatures of the ocean!"

The army laughed at such foolish babble. "Surely he's gone mad," whispered one soldier to another. "Enough!" cried Taro. "Behold! Fish, I command you: rise to the water's edge!" The creature saved by Taro was listening to the man, swam to the surface, and created dazzling *mie* with its fins, tail, and mouth. The opposing general laughed and attributed it to nothing more than coincidence. "Witness!" Taro cried. "Life of the ocean, I command you: rise to the water's edge!"

At that moment, the millions of creatures that inhabited the ocean came to the surface at the magic fish's command. The army gasped at the octopi, sea horses, eels, and jellyfish that danced *mie* hauntingly on the water's surface. Taro then turned to the men and said, "More? Behold the final charge. Fish, I command you: dance in the air!" The millions of creatures jumped out of the water and began swimming in the sky. The soldiers, believing now in Taro's incantations, dropped their swords in horror and fled from the bizarre sight. Even the opposing general himself outran his swiftest man. "There is evil magic here! Retreat!"

Taro laughed as the army disappeared from his sight. He turned to the creatures inhabiting the sky and gently spoke, "Fish, I thank you. Return to your home." The sea life dropped into the ocean with a mighty splash and swam to its lower depths. But the magic fish remained and bowed to Taro. Taro returned the courtesy.

"We have saved each other—and that makes us equal," the fish said. "But I will repay the debt with a final gift." Two seahorses brought a small treasure chest from the ocean and placed it at Taro's feet. "Pearls?" thought Taro. As he opened the chest, the magic fish explained, "Inside are the greatest gifts I can give you at this time—fresh water, food, and a pillow for your comfort. For what good are riches of the world if the body, mind, and soul are not nourished?"

The magic fish disappeared into the ocean, never to be seen again. Taro drank, ate, and rested on the pillow, reflecting on the wisdom of the creature that saved his life.

Session Design for "Taro and the Magic Fish"

Materials

- small drum
- illustrations of ancient Japanese warriors
- illustrations of underwater life
- cassette tape player
- cassette tape of Japanese flute or Kabuki music

Story Drama Activities

1. MOTIVATE children by doing one or more of the following:

a. Show illustrations of ancient Japanese warriors. Discuss the early dynasties of Japan and the battles fought for power.

b. Show illustrations of unusual and exotic underwater life.

c. Play Kabuki music from Japan. Ask players from which country they believe the music to be; if they respond correctly, ask "How do you know that?"

d. Explain the term *mie* and how it resembles a "still picture" or an actor's dynamic pose from the Japanese Kabuki theatre. Ask for volunteers from class to model poses for the class as the leader guides them.

2. PRESENT the story: Playing Kabuki or Japanese flute music softly under the retelling is an effective method of creating a sense of period.

3. DRAMATIZE the story:

a. Ask players to find their own space in the cleared room. Describe the *mie* as explained in the introduction to "Taro and the Magic Fish," or as demonstrated during the motivation. "When you hear the drumbeat, pose yourself as if you're a Japanese warrior with a sword—no movement, just a frozen picture." Observe and assess. "Now try a different pose shaping your body in a completely different way." Ask players to explore a different *mie* with each drumbeat the leader makes. Experiment with a few more poses, sidecoaching as needed: "Make your legs part of the *mie*"; "Don't forget that your face should also be part of the *mie*." Ask players to relax and assess their work.

b. Ask players to think about one of the creatures in the story that could have emerged from the ocean, and tell students to "begin shaping your body to create that creature and move slowly through the room as if you were under water—slowly, slowly without touching anyone else." Observe and assess. Again, ask players to shape themselves into several *mie* as sea creatures, accompanied by five drumbeats. Observe and assess. Ask players, "What did you do to make the creature *mie* different from the human soldier *mie*?"

c. Organize the class into split-half groups, one group as ocean life, the other as soldiers. Select or ask for one volunteer from each group to portray the magic fish and the general of the opposing army (neither role should be gender-specific). The leader will portray Taro. Work with the child selected to play the magic fish as the children portraying the soldiers and other creatures sit to the side and observe.

d. The leader and child as the magic fish review the scenario for the first part of the story. Establish the central part of the space as the seashore and practice how the fish will enter the action, what dialogue will be exchanged, and how the fish will leave the action.

e. Direct the army group to find a way of entering the action of the story. If the leader is comfortable, the child selected to play the general can beat the drum to bring the army into the action (the central space of the room). Children sometimes suggest using *mie* as they approach the area. Organize the group so they are on one side of the area (the shore). Review with the child portraying the general the basic sequence of action and dialogue between Taro and him.

f. Practice the next unit in which the magic fish appears and creates *mie* for the army. Then practice the unit in which all the creatures enter the action on their side of the room (the ocean) and form their *mie* on the water and in the air. Organize how and where the children portraying the soldiers will go when they retreat and their portion of the dramatization is completed.

g. The leader works with the children portraying the creatures, practicing how they will return to the sea and leave the action. The children portraying the magic fish and two seahorses are then guided through their unit of action for bringing the treasure chest to Taro.

h. Ask players if there are any questions before the units are assembled for a complete playing. Review any cautionary guidelines and notes for an effective playing (e.g., no physical contact, believability, and commitment to the drama). If possible, play Japanese music softly to enhance the mood for the playing.

i. The leader enters the action as Taro, thirsty and hungry, searching for water and food. The units, as practiced above, are then played through nonstop for the dramatization. If some children are inclined to break the mood of the drama through an inappropriate verbal comment, the leader may consider whether stopping the playing is worthwhile to discuss the remark. (As an example from one of my sessions, when the creatures appeared, one of the soldiers in the army shouted "Sushi!", causing other children to laugh. That comment merited the stopping of the action.)

4. ASSESS the dramatization:

a. The leader offers his observations to children on their believability and commitment to the playing. Mention the level of seriousness and integrity maintained throughout the drama.

b. Discuss how movement played an important part in the dramatization. Ask children how easy or difficult it may have been to use their bodies for the playing. Discuss what kind of training might be needed for an actor portraying these characters on a stage.

c. If interest is high, replay the story incorporating suggestions mentioned during the assessment. For maximum learning, ask players to switch roles for the second playing so that soldiers now become creatures and vice versa.

d. Discuss how the story might be dramatized if puppets were used instead of people for creatures. If interest is high, have children create their own rod puppets for the underwater life and dramatize the story in a future session.

Social Studies Follow-Up

1. Locate Japan on a globe or map.

2. Discuss how the story's ending has an environmental theme. Discuss countries or cultures that consider the environment a prominent part of their existence.

3. The story's action does not mention a specific time period in Japanese history. Discuss when Japan was at war during its early dynasties. What were the motivations for these wars?

Language Arts/Literature Follow-Up

1. Read Katherine Paterson's *The Master Puppeteer* (New York: Thomas Y. Crowell Co., 1975). Discuss the life of a puppeteer in Japan's Bunraku theatre, as depicted in the novel. Dramatize scenes from the work that lend themselves to improvisation.

2. Watch a videotape of traditional Japanese theatre forms, such as Kabuki or Bunraku. Discuss how the styles of these theatre forms are different from the styles usually produced in the United States. Discuss how "Taro and the Magic Fish" might be staged as a Kabuki or Bunraku presentation. Dramatize the story again, incorporating selected elements (movement, sound effects, etc.) from the traditional Japanese theatre.

3. The character of Taro is featured in other Japanese folktales. Locate and read these stories. "Taro and the Magic Fish" was created by a Japanese American family that selected and combined elements from traditional Japanese stories and the Japanese Kabuki theatre. Find elements or motifs from the authentic Japanese tales that found their

way into this story created in the twentieth century. Dramatize those stories that lend themselves to improvisation.

"THE TEN FARMERS"

The approach to this story for children in grades 4–6 is holistic. The tale is used as a springboard for improvisational story creation rather than dramatization, much like the session designs for "The Warning" in Chapter Four and "A Holy Cat" in Chapter Six.

This improvisational session asks children to think about the nature of good and evil. The leader, as facilitator of the drama, assumes a role not included in the story—a monk. The character is used in the session to set the problem in motion and generate discussion and debate. The direction the story takes depends on the children's decisions. The leader plays a critical role in extending and challenging children's thinking and assumptions. What may appear as an abstract, philosophical session is actually a drama woven with tension and a surprise ending for the participants.

Many years ago there were ten farm workers, who were all traveling together. They were surprised by a heavy thunderstorm, and all took refuge in a half-ruined temple. But the thunder drew ever nearer, and so great was the storm that the air trembled about them, while the lightning flashed around and around the temple in a great circle.

The farmers were all badly frightened, and decided that there must be a sinner among them, whom the lightning was trying to strike. To find out which one of them it might be, they agreed to hang up their straw hats outside the door. He whose hat was blown away would have to go outside and let himself be struck by lightning.

But one of the ten farmers protested. "Surely not one among us is without some sin," said he. "But if any one of us is without sin, surely that innocent man has no fear of death." But the others would not listen to him.

No sooner were all the hats outside, than one of them was blown away. Sure enough, it was the hat of the one farmer who had protested. Then all the others laughed, and pushed the unlucky owner out of doors without pity. But as soon as he had left, the lightning ceased circling, and struck the temple with a crash.

For the one that the rest had pushed out had been the only really good person among them, and for his sake the lightning had spared the temple. Thus the evil nine farmers had to pay with their lives for their cruelty to their companion.

Session Design for "The Ten Farmers"

Materials

- cassette tape of continuous thunderstorm sound effects
- cassette tape player

Story Drama Activities

1. MOTIVATE children by doing one or more of the following:

a. If the class has had some experience with story drama, explain that this session will be approached differently: "Instead of me telling a story first, this time the way the story progresses and ends will depend on where *you* take the action. The setting, characters, and problem will be presented to you as we work through the session, but the way the story ends depends on the kinds of decisions you make as we go on. Listen carefully because later I'll be playing a role that will help you get the information you need to push the drama forward."

b. Push all desks, chairs, and tables to the side of the room to permit work in the center area. Play the cassette tape of thunderstorm sound effects; if possible, dim the lights in the room. Ask players what kinds of moods are evoked by these effects.

2. PRESENT the story: It is suggested that the story not be shared with children at the beginning of the session but at the end. The leader uses the story as the framework for the improvisation to explore the themes of good and evil.

3. DRAMATIZE the story:

a. Ask players to get into small groups of four or five. If the class is open to forming small groups with a mix of boys and girls, encourage them to do so. "Each person in your group is a member of the same community that works on a farm. You might all be related, like a family, or perhaps you're just good friends who work together. You've been working the land in China, but you've gotten caught in this terrible thunderstorm. No umbrellas, nothing to hide under; it's just you and your group in an open field. With each group working in its own space and without any talking, show through your face and body how fierce the storm is and how you might try to protect each other from the rain. Go." Observe the work and sidecoach, as needed, reinforcing that no verbal work be done and encouraging serious commitment to the activity. As the sound effects continue, sidecoach to players, "Walk *slowly* throughout the room with your group, showing that the rain, thunder, and lightning are overwhelming and you're trying to find a place to take shelter from the storm. Again, no sounds; let your movements and face say what you might be thinking and feeling. Go." Observe and reinforce such guidelines as moving slowly. Once commitment is observed, sidecoach. "Through the pouring rain your group spots a small building nearby. Show how you would react at seeing a place to take shelter. Come inside and take refuge. Wipe the water off you and try to get dry. I'll be stepping into role soon. Talk to each other to see if everybody is all right." Observe the dialogue exchanged between students.

b. The leader now takes on the role of a monk who takes care of the temple. The basic goal is to evoke an aura of mystery and tension by the character's demeanor and vocal tone. What follows is an example of the kind of dialogue I used with a group of fourth graders: "Who are you? What are doing in this temple? Answer me." Listen to children's responses and improvise in role to whatever questions they may ask. Some may ask about the leader's character. He can respond that he is a monk who is in the temple for meditation. After introductory dialogue has been exchanged, or if some children generate responses that are inconsistent with the seriousness of the piece, the leader can respond coldly, "This is a sacred place. It will keep you safe from the storm and you're welcome to stay. But reverence and respect *will* be shown here." Stare at the players in an intimidating manner. "Please be quiet while I meditate."

c. The leader sets himself away from the group as if in meditation. The leader then sighs deeply or moans as if in pain. The intent is to spark attention and curiosity from the students. The monk turns to the children and states, "There is . . . an evil presence here. I feel it. Some of you have done something very wrong. And the thunderstorm is punishment for your wickedness. But the evil ones are mixed with the good, and it's difficult to feel which ones are which. I have thought a lot about what is good and what is evil. Have you?" The leader improvises with children on the nature of good and evil. Depending on the grade level, some children will use specific examples from their own experiences rather than discuss the subject on an abstract, philosophical level. The leader, however, should not be hesitant to ask complex questions to get children thinking about the "greys" of good and evil: "How do we know a person's good?" "What makes people evil?" "How can someone be good and evil at the same time?" Continue this discussion until an appropriate stopping point has been reached.

d. The leader may break the discussion abruptly and re-spark interest by saying, "Silence. Silence. I am feeling something new. The evil ones must be removed. For the sake of the good, the evil ones must leave. The evil ones must face the fury of the thunderstorm outside so the good can be protected inside the temple. Otherwise the lightning will destroy us all. Who will leave? Who are the evil ones in here?" If children begin accusing each other (with imaginary or actual rationales) the leader can counter their accusations with, "Were you there?" "What may be evil to you may be good to someone else." "The evil ones can disguise themselves as good people." "Why are some so quick to accuse and some so silent?" The purpose of the leader's challenges is to assist players with seeing the complexities of an issue. Above all the leader should not demean a student response, but probe the issue or response even further by examining several points of view.

e. If whole group discussion becomes unmanageable, the leader can steer the discussion into small groups by suggesting, "You came into this temple as families and friends. Is there one or more in your group who is evil? Who will leave to face the fury of the thunderstorm so the good can be saved? The lightning is getting dangerously close and we have little time left." The leader suggests that each group should decide who among them will leave the temple. As the groups discuss among themselves, the leader can circulate among the children, in role, ensuring that "respect" is maintained inside the temple. Tension can be added by such sidecoaching in role as, "The thunder is getting louder; we must make our decisions soon."

f. When the leader observes that small groups have reached some kind of decision (and some groups may not have reached any decision, which is acceptable), the leader then asks each group to explain to the others who has been identified as evil and why. Group response and rationales will vary. Some may have been accused and selected by others. Some will openly admit to their "evil" and volunteer to leave. Others may choose to maintain their bond, leave the temple together and face the consequences. (In one session, the entire class decided that the monk was evil and *he* should be the one to leave.) Whatever choices have been made by the groups should be accepted.

g. Those identified as evil are escorted by the leader to one side of the room. They are asked, "Are you ready to face the thunderstorm?" Student responses are acknowledged by the leader, and they are told to sit "outside" (the side of the room) and await their fate. The leader returns to the ones who remain in the temple and asks them, "Do you feel that the evil is gone?" After listening to student responses, the leader then concludes the session: "From my master's teachings I learned a story about good and evil." The leader then shares the tale of "The Ten Farmers" with the group, pointedly referring to those who stayed inside the temple as the ones who will be destroyed by lightning.

4. ASSESS the dramatization: The focus of assessment for this session is primarily reflection on student feelings rather than assessment of drama skills.

a. The leader announces he is out of role as the monk and asks the entire class to sit in a circle. Ask players for their initial reactions to the ending of the story. The ones expelled from the temple and those who remained inside may each have different reactions.

b. The leader shares some of the remarks or comments he recalls from children's dialogue about the nature of good and evil. Assess what children may have gained through their discussions about the complexities of the topic.

c. Ask players to describe how they felt about the character of the monk. "When I was playing that role, how did you feel about the monk's challenges to your opinions and responses?"

d. If traditional story dramatization has been conducted with the class, ask players to describe how this method of improvising the story was different from dramatizing a story they heard first. Ask students to describe why this approach was easier or more difficult.

e. Discuss possible directions or alternative endings the improvisation might have taken. Discuss how player and leader choices affect or influence the structure of drama.

Social Studies Follow-Up

1. Locate China on a globe or map.

2. Identify the primary religion practiced in China. Discuss how "The Ten Farmers" may reflect aspects of the culture's religious/spiritual beliefs.

3. Identify historical or contemporary figures who are generally portrayed as or considered good (humanitarian, philanthropic, etc.) and evil (notorious, criminal, etc.) (e.g., Mother Teresa, Adolph Hitler).

Specify the personality characteristics and actions that contribute to their reputations. Identify historical figures who may be considered good by some people, evil by others (e.g., Christopher Columbus from different cultural perspectives). Identify why their personality characteristics and actions may be interpreted differently. Finally, discuss why some people may hold differing opinions about historic figures (e.g., Why do some people revere Adolph Hitler? Why do some condemn Rev. Dr. Martin Luther King, Jr.?).

Language Arts/Literature Follow-Up

1. Discuss irony as a literary device. Identify what is ironic in "The Ten Farmers."

2. Discuss the characteristics of a protagonist and antagonist. Relate how the problem or theme of good versus evil in literature is realized through characters or situations.

3. Write an original story or poem on "Good and Evil," based on the discussion and improvisation generated from the dramatization. Dramatize those works that lend themselves to improvisation.

4. As school policy allows, compare "The Ten Farmers" to the Biblical story in John 8:1–11 (casting the first stone). Discuss the similarities and differences between the two stories.

6

Stories from the African and African American Canons

"FATIMA AND THE SNAKE"

C. K. Ganyo, a dance instructor at Arizona State University and a native to Africa, told this story to student Kenneth Bass who told it in one of my classes. I told it to a group of children and teachers in New Orleans and one of the arts specialists, John Lehon, transcribed the story for documentation. The African American children with whom I worked may have passed this story on to other children and adults in Louisiana. Such is the nature of the oral tradition. As with all stories passed from one person to another, "Fatima and the Snake" is retold below based on how John and I recalled and reshaped it.

This tale from Ghana is rich with symbolism but appropriate for grades K–3. It is both a cautionary and rite-of-passage tale and a story that explains the origin of snake bracelets. Older children with previous drama experience can explore the dramatization through simultaneous pair playing as Fatima and her mother for the first half of the story.

In Ghana they tell of a girl named Fatima. She was not a patient one, and she often did not obey the rules her mother asked her to follow.

When Fatima was weaving baskets her mother would say, "You must

131

be patient as you twist and press the grass into place, or the basket will be no use to anyone." But Fatima did not like weaving baskets, especially in the hot sun. She wanted to play in the cool shade of the trees. So Fatima hurried through her work, and the basket had many gaps where things could fall through. Her mother frowned when she saw what Fatima had done and said, "Why can't you be more patient? You have wasted your time and this fine grass on a useless basket that won't hold a thing."

When Fatima was sent to the field to dig yams, her mother warned her to work slowly and carefully with the pointed stick because it could easily pierce the yam and ruin it. But Fatima did not like to dig for yams. She wanted to get out of the hot sun and play in the cool shade of the trees. So she quickly and carelessly dug the yams, and many were broken. Her mother sighed when she saw what Fatima had done and said, "Why can't you be more patient? These yams are all in pieces; now we cannot eat them. You must learn to listen to what I tell you."

When Fatima would help her mother pierce and string beads for necklaces her mother would say, "You must be careful as you push the point through the bead or the bead will split and be ruined." But Fatima wanted to finish quickly so she could play in the cool shade of the trees. Many beautiful beads were broken as she hurried through her work. Her mother shook her head when she saw what her daughter had done and said, "Fatima, you have broken more beads than you have on the necklace. Why aren't you more patient about your work?"

And Fatima said, "I don't want to work, I want to play in the cool shade of the trees."

"Fatima, you're too little to go into the jungle by yourself. There is too much danger in there. Stay home where it's safe."

But Fatima did not obey. When her mother was busy cooking, Fatima ran into the jungle to play. She walked through thick grass, hanging vines and prickly bushes. When she stopped she realized she was lost. On a tree branch above her there appeared a strange creature she had never seen before. It was long, round, and made a strange hissing sound. It lowered its head toward Fatima and said, "Hello, little one."

"Hello," Fatima said softly, still uncertain of this strange creature. "What are you?"

"The humans call me Snake."

"I've never seen a . . . snake before," Fatima said, fascinated by the slowly moving beast.

The snake said to her, "Would you like to feel my skin?"

"Oh, yes," she said. Fatima reached out to touch the scaly hide and shuddered, "It's cold and rough."

"Would you like to feel my tongue against your cheek?"

"Oh, yes," said Fatima. The snake slithered closer and licked her face with its quickly darting tongue. She giggled and said, "It tickles."

"Would you like to feel my big, white teeth?"

"Oh yes," said Fatima. She reached inside the snake's open mouth to touch the long, white fangs. But when her hand was inside the snake snapped its jaws, pierced Fatima's wrist, then slithered quickly back onto the tree branch above her. Fatima let out a scream as she saw her own blood spill to the ground. She ran through the jungle crying for help, and by luck alone returned to her own village. By the time she reached home to tell her mother what had happened, Fatima fainted from the snake's poison running through her body.

Fatima was sick for many days. She tossed and turned with endless dreams as her mother kept watch by her side. And while Fatima was recovering from the poison, her mother made a bracelet and coiled it around her daughter's wrist.

When Fatima awoke from her fever she felt her mother hugging her closely. They kissed each other, both glad Fatima was alive. Her mother said, "While you were asleep I made this bracelet to remind you of the dangers out there." Fatima saw that the bracelet coiled around her wrist looked just like a snake. And it helped her remember there are dangers in the world, and she should listen to the wisdom of her mother who had already faced them.

Session Design for "Fatima and the Snake"

Materials

- aluminum foil sheets, cut into twelve-inch lengths, one for each student
- illustration of a snake with large fangs
- snake bracelet

Story Drama Activities

1. MOTIVATE children by doing one or more of the following:

a. Discuss why we have rules to follow; explain how adults set most rules because of danger children may not know.

b. Show an illustration of a large snake with fangs and ask about the potential danger.

c. Show a snake bracelet and ask children how this piece of jewelry may have originated.

2. PRESENT the story: One of the techniques I saw a storyteller employ with this tale is to mold and shape a piece of aluminum foil into a snake bracelet as the story is being told. By the conclusion of the story, the bracelet is coiled around the storyteller's wrist.

3. DRAMATIZE the story:

    a. Inform players they will all be playing the role of Fatima while the leader takes the role of the mother. For the initial activities children may work seated at their desks or seated in their own space in a room cleared of desks and chairs. In role as the mother, tell children, "Fatima, here are strips of dried grass. Start working on weaving your basket, but go slow. Because if it's not woven tight then the basket won't be any good. Now get to work." Announce that the leader is out of role as the mother and sidecoach players on their weaving: "Pick up strips of dried grass and show through your hands that you're trying to make a basket. But remember that it's hot outside, so try to show you're weaving a basket while you're trying to stay cool." Observe the players' work and assess. "As Fatima went on with her weaving she got more and more careless. Now try to show you're weaving a basket while it's hot and you're really not too interested in doing this work." Observe and sidecoach what you find effective.

    b. Announce that the leader is now entering the playing as the mother. Encourage dialogue from children by setting up a conflict and asking questions: "Fatima, let me see your work. Why, look at this basket, it's got holes all through it. Why didn't you take your time like I told you?" If children respond to the questioning, improvise and exchange dialogue. Proceed to the next unit of play through transition: "If you can't do well at weaving, let's get you started on digging for yams. Pick up that long stick. Poke through the dirt until the yam comes loose then pull up the yam. But poke the ground slowly and carefully, or else you'll pierce right through it. I'll come back to see how many you've dug." Announce that the leader is now out of role and sidecoach players as they work: "Show through your arms and hands that you're using the stick to dig for yams. But also try to show how hot it is and that you'd rather be playing instead of working." Observe and assess. "Now show through your actions that you've pierced and broken several yams. Try to show how Fatima might be feeling after her mother told her to be careful. I'm coming back now as your mother. 'Fatima, let me see how many yams you've dug. Oh, Fatima! They're all in pieces. Why didn't you listen to what I told you?'" Dialogue with children as they initiate responses.

c. Continue with the same sequence and exchange described above for stringing the beads. Encourage children to work for detail in their pantomime as they string beads onto thread.

d. With all players out of role discuss what feelings might be held by the characters of Fatima and her mother after these three failed attempts. Discuss the playing of the next unit between Fatima and Snake. Ask players to walk around the space as you sidecoach them into the jungle: "Begin walking through the room as if you're sneaking away, glad that you're free from all the work you have to do. Show through your face that you're looking around at new things you've never seen before, and show through your body that you're walking through tall grass and low hanging vines." Observe and assess. "Now show through your face and body that you don't know where you are, that you're lost, that it's starting to get dark and you're worried." Ask players to gather back in a circle. Share what was effective about the work.

e. Discuss the next unit of play: the leader will take the role of Fatima while the children portray the Snake. Ask players how the character might be created through movement; practice whatever formation they suggest. Encourage the Snake to move around the space and hiss softly. Ask players how the dialogue might be exchanged between Fatima and the Snake—one person at the head of the Snake speaking? all parts of the Snake allowed to speak? Adopt whatever the group decides. Review the sequence of actions made between Fatima and the Snake (feeling the skin, the tongue against her cheek, biting the wrist). Ask players how these three actions might be dramatized without physical contact and practice what the group decides. Decide where and how the Snake will "enter" and "exit" the playing space during the unit for a proper sense of beginning and closure to the unit.

f. The leader prompts the Snake to enter the playing area. The leader as Fatima dialogues with the Snake accordingly. The dialogue exchange from the story may be used as a model for improvisation, but by no means does it need to be adhered to faithfully or committed to memory. When Fatima is bitten, the leader reacts accordingly and leaves the playing area while the Snake exits the area. Gather players back into a circle and assess their work as the Snake.

g. Discuss the next unit of play: children, as Fatima, will come to the leader, as the mother, and tell their story of what happened in the jungle, making sure they tell the story in Fatima's agitated state.

Discuss how the players might "lose consciousness" as Fatima did without hurting themselves or each other when they drop to the ground. Encourage slow motion and practice the sequence before dramatizing the unit. Also encourage children to "lose consciousness" gradually rather than dropping rapidly to the floor. Dramatize the unit with the leader prompting through questions: "Fatima, there you are—where have you been?" "There's blood on your wrist, what happened?" "What's wrong with you—why are you sleepy?"

h. As players lie on the ground, step out of role and softly sidecoach children to image what Fatima may be dreaming: "Lie still and quiet. Think about all the things Fatima did on this day, all the things she worked on, touched and felt, and try to mix them up together like dreams sometimes do." Allow some silent time for players to image Fatima's dream. "The poison in your body might be making your brain think funny thoughts, but your mother is holding you and taking care of you while you're sick. You're getting better each day, and one day, finally, you wake up." The leader as the mother dialogues with all children as Fatima: "How are you feeling, sweet one?" Encourage players to tell you what they "dreamt." After dreams have been shared, tell children that, while they were asleep, you made them a bracelet to remind them of the Snake and the danger it can be. Close the dramatization by affirming that the mother loves Fatima very much and is glad she's alive.

4. ASSESS the dramatization:

a. Ask players which portions of the dramatization were enjoyed most.

b. Share with children what observations the leader made about their work. Offer what was effective about their dramatization with emphasis on dialogue and adherence to any rules established for playing.

c. Ask all children to construct a snake bracelet out of a piece of aluminum foil. Roll or fold the foil square into a single length and shape one end like a snake's head. Coil the snake around the wrist to hold it in place.

Social Studies Follow-Up

1. Locate Africa and Ghana on a globe or map.

2. Discuss the people of Ghana and their culture.

3. Discuss how the oral tradition and folklore in Africa are used to pass accumulated knowledge and wisdom from one generation to the

next. Discuss why stories were used to transmit this knowledge rather than transmission of the knowledge through facts.

Language Arts/Literature Follow-Up

1. This story was collected from an oral source and, to the author's knowledge, does not exist elsewhere in print. Retell this story to another friend to keep the story alive and spreading in the oral tradition.

2. Compare this story to "Little Eight John" (in this chapter). How are Fatima and Little Eight John's characters and problems similar? different?

3. Discuss the messages and themes this story makes to its audience.

4. Ideas for what Fatima might have dreamt were discussed during the playing. Write a fantasy story titled "Fatima's Dream" and draw an illustration to accompany it. If possible, dramatize these dream stories in class.

"ANANSI AND THE STICKY MAN"

This African-origin precursor of Joel Chandler Harris' tar baby tale is appropriate for dramatization in grades K–3. Anansi stories are well known and available in several versions. Many also lend themselves to story drama, and the tale below is just one of such stories.

Anansi—who gave us all stories—doesn't like this one to be told. That gluttonous, lazy spider once robbed the food out of his own family's mouths.

All of them feasted on sweet, sweet vegetables growing in a nearby field. But it wasn't enough for that greedy Anansi. "I must have more— I must have it all."

So that no-good eight legs pretended to die, and put the burden of burying him on his wife and all his sons. They cried and cried and put Anansi to rest in the field of sweet, sweet vegetables. And that was what he wanted all along. "I now have more—I now have it all."

When the stars came out he crawled out of his grave and he ate, and he ate, and he ate. When the sun came up he crawled back to his grave and he slept, and he slept, and he slept. Anansi's family came daily for food, but saw there was more missing than what they were eating. "Someone is robbing us," the widow spider cried. "We're hungry, we're starving," her little sons replied.

So they made a trap to catch the one who stole their sweet, sweet vegetables. From gum they formed an icky man—a tricky man—a sticky man. They set it out in the middle of the field and left it there to catch the thief.

When nighttime fell Anansi crawled out, and he ate, and he ate, and he ate. "I now have more—I now have it all." Then the sticky man's shadow fell on Anansi in the bright white moonlight glow. The spider gasped and turned suddenly around. "Thief!" cried Anansi. "Get out of this field. All vegetables here are mine." But the sticky man stood silent, silent, which frightened the greedy spider.

"What you need is a slap for your senses. Take that," Anansi shouted. But when the spider's leg struck the sticky man it stuck and held fast to its face. "Let go!" demanded the spider, "or you'll feel another whack." Anansi kept to his word and slapped the man once more. And there stood Anansi with two of his eight legs fastened tightly to the sticky man's head.

"Want more, do you?" the angry spider laughed. And a third then a fourth leg came across the icky man. Five, then six, then seven, then eight. All legs were now attached as the spider stood struggling to set himself free. "Help me!" screamed Anansi, as he and the sticky man crashed to the ground. And the spider's head and fat, fat body were glued to the icky man's torso. Spider rolled and wiggled but couldn't get free, and laid there all night in the sticky man's grasp.

When morning came the spider clan went in the field to check their trap. They found their father breathless on the ground with the sticky man lying on top. "Papa!" cried Anansi's sons. "Husband!" cried the wife. They set him loose from the sticky man's grasp and learned the story of Anansi's deceit.

When word of the tale was spread to others they laughed at the spider's folly. So embarrassed was Anansi at having been caught that he crawled in a corner to hide in shame.

So if you want to see a spider, look not in the light. The spider hides in darkness to this day.

Session Design for "Anansi and the Sticky Man"

Materials

- glue or paste
- illustration or photograph of a spider

Story Drama Activities

1. MOTIVATE children by doing one or more of the following:
   a. Discuss the properties of glue or paste. Ask what happens when it gets on one's skin.

   b. Show an illustration of a spider; discuss the properties of spider webs. Ask why the spider does not get stuck on its own web.

   c. Ask players why spiders are generally found in secluded areas (corners, darkness, etc.). Segue into the telling of the tale.

2. PRESENT the story: A straightforward retelling of the story is sufficient before the dramatization.

3. DRAMATIZE the story:
   a. Ask students to find their own space in the room. In ensemble, ask players to shape their bodies as if they were spiders: "There's no right or wrong way, but explore how your legs and arms become part of the spider. Move slowly across the space as you think your spider character would crawl." Observe and assess the work. "Find a place to stop and relax. When some spiders die, their legs might curl up and they'll lie on their backs. Without any sounds, reshape your body as if your spider is dead." Observe and assess. Ask players to relax.

   (The next unit of action dramatizes the funeral for Anansi. If the leader feels this unit may be inappropriate for her group, she may proceed directly to **c.**)

   b. Tell players the leader will be playing in role as Anansi's widow, and the class will be Anansi's children. Announce in a matter-of-fact voice, "Children, now that your father's gone, we're on our own. We'll have to bury him someplace where he'll be happy. Where do you think your father would like his final resting place?" If children present ideas which were not part of the story scenario, acknowledge them but sway the group toward the vegetable field. Ask players what kind of ceremony would be appropriate for their father's funeral and facilitate the dramatization of their ideas. (It is recommended that no one play the dead Anansi; keep the character "invisible." Depending on leader goals, ideas could be focused on African cultural elements with contemporary or non-African elements avoided. The leader in role can also encourage children to "show respect" for their dead father if behavior becomes erratic.) As children dramatize the ceremony encourage them to keep spiderlike movements. After the ceremony assess the players' work.

c. Ask players to find their own space in the room and shape themselves into the "dead" Anansi. If possible, dim the lights in the room. Take players through a narrative pantomime in the vegetable field: "Night has come, and you slowly uncurl yourself and crawl out of your grave on your eight legs. Look around to make sure no one sees you, and start feasting on the vegetables." Observe and sidecoach, as needed. "After eating all night your stomach is full. Morning is here, so crawl back into your grave, curl up, and sleep for the day." Turn the lights back on and assess the players' work.

d. The leader announces she will play in role as Anansi's widow while all students portray her children for the unit on discovering the missing vegetables. "Look at this field. Almost everything's gone and there's hardly anything left for us. We're going to starve. Who's been robbing us?" Dialogue with children if they initiate ideas. "We've got to put a stop to this and catch that thief. Smart children, what shall we do?" Acknowledge ideas from children, even if not mentioned in the story. Bring resolution to the sticky man idea and ask players how it will be created. Facilitate its creation, encouraging as much group participation as possible. (In one class, everyone chewed imaginary gum, then pieced it together into the shape of a man.)

e. Before the next unit is dramatized, ask players how they might show their hand stuck on an imaginary head: "Pretend you're giving the sticky man a slap and show through your face and body that it's stuck. Go." Observe and assess. "Now slap the imaginary head with your other hand and that one gets stuck—make sure you show through your hands that there's a head shape." Observe and assess. If available space and soft flooring allow, have children practice getting their legs stuck on the imaginary sticky man. Discourage falling if space is not available and emphasize that no physical contact is to be made with anyone. The leader shares that she will be taking the children through a narrative pantomime of the final unit, then playing in role as Anansi's wife after Anansi gets completely stuck. She will free him from the sticky man then laugh at Anansi, who should then crawl to a space to "hide" in shame.

f. Players find their own space in the room and curl back into Anansi's sleeping position. Dim the lights if possible. Prompt players to look toward the leader when they interact with the sticky man. The leader narrates the opening action: "Night has come and Anansi wakes up, uncurls, and crawls out of his grave to eat the vegetables. But you see someone in the field, and you demand to know who he is and what he's doing here." Sidecoach children to speak to the imaginary man. "Anansi gets no answer so he slaps the man once and gets stuck. He slaps him again and gets stuck. Now a third slap with his leg; a fourth slap with the other leg; and Anansi struggles and struggles but can't get free." Sidecoach players to respect each other's space, as needed. "The sun rises, and Anansi's widow comes to the vegetable field." Turn the lights on in the room and continue: "Husband! Is that you? We thought you were dead!" Dialogue with children as they provide answers to leader questions such as, "Where were you all day?" or "Why did you do this to your family?" If players ask to be freed from the sticky man, the leader can retort in role, "Not yet, I've got some questions to ask you." The leader can chastise Anansi for his trick, and begin laughing as she pulls the sticky man off him. As children crawl off to hide the leader might continue laughing with such dialogue as, "Wait until everyone hears about this. You should have seen yourself!" Drop out of role and ask children to gather back in a circle.

4. **ASSESS the dramatization:**
   a. Assess the players' ability to improvise and follow directions for dramatizing the final unit.

   b. Ask players to describe the challenges of creating spiderlike movements and pantomiming the sticky man.

   c. Ask players to describe the emotions Anansi felt throughout the story with particular emphasis on "getting caught." Ask players to describe instances from their own lives when they lied.

Social Studies Follow-Up

1. Locate Africa on a globe or map.

2. Discuss why a spider became such a prominent character in selected African folktales.

3. This story explains "why" spiders live in dark corners. Discuss why cultures developed "why" or "how" stories to explain things found in nature.

4. Discuss how animal characters in folk literature represent human personality traits or behavior. What traits or actions displayed by Anansi in "Anansi and the Sticky Man" are also found among humans?

Language Arts/Literature Follow-Up

1. Read other stories that feature Anansi the Spider. Dramatize these stories in class.

2. Read another version of "Anansi and the Sticky Man" and compare it to Joel Chandler Harris' "The Wonderful Tar-Baby" (if the school or community feels Harris' version is appropriate for their children) or Virginia Hamilton's "Doc Rabbit, Bruh Fox, and Tar Baby" in *The People Could Fly* (New York: Alfred A. Knopf, 1985). Examine what motifs or elements from the African story made their way into the African American version.

3. Read other "why" stories from the African canons of folk literature. Compare these to "why" or "how" stories from other cultures.

4. Read several Anansi stories and several Coyote stories from the Native American canons. Compare the characters of Anansi and Coyote and extract their similarities. Discuss why characters with similar traits would evolve in the folklore from these two diverse cultures.

"A HOLY CAT"

This story is dramatized in a holistic manner. Players are asked to explore the themes of the story rather than dramatize the action after hearing the tale. This fable focuses on trust and the nature of animals (symbols for humans) trying to change their ways. If there are concerns over the religious content of the story, these themes can be underplayed while the conflicts between the animals are stressed.

Children in grades 2–4 portray the rodents in the story while the leader plays in role as the cat.

A cat goes on a pilgrimage

A well-known cat from a certain alley in a town in North Africa decided to go on a pilgrimage to the Holy City. When he told the other cats about his unusual plan there was so much talk about it down the alleyways and on the street corners that the rats and mice heard about it too. They all wondered what the cat was thinking of.

When the cat came back after his journey he was quite changed, and went around being very religious. He wore a white turban and a white flowing burnoose, just like any other Muslim scholar, and instead of stalking rats and mice he would stand on his favorite street corner praying and reading. Sometimes he would walk around with his eyes half-closed and his nose in the air, with his mind obviously on higher things.

The rats were puzzled, and to find out what was going on the chief rat went to pay the cat his compliments and hope he had a good pilgrimage. When the chief rat arrived the cat had a pair of reading glasses on, and was reading the Holy Book.

The rat bowed. "Good morning, reverend cat. I have been sent by the rodent community to pay our respects to your learned reverence, and to ask what wisdom you wish to impart to us from your trip to the Holy Place."

"Welcome, rodent chief. Yes, I have learned much at the Holy City. I have learned to read and pray. I have learned to love my fellow creatures and respect their freedom. I have learned that it is wicked to kill rats and mice and eat them. I used to hunt them for food, and sometimes I even enjoyed it, but this unfortunate habit of mine is a thing of the past. You rats and mice may run and frolic wherever you will. In my new holy life I eat only dates and milk and bread."

The rat bowed again and hurried back to tell the others the news. They weren't sure how to take it, but decided they would watch and see if they could observe any of these changes for themselves.

Next morning two of them were having a quiet sip at a gutter when they saw the cat coming down the alley toward them, walking very slowly, with his head in the air. He didn't seem to see the rats at all. He was reading in the Holy Book, learning bits from it, muttering the words over and over to himself. Then he stopped and took out a piece of bread from his burnoose, and stood there nibbling it for a minute or two, before he went on.

The same thing happened the next day to some other rats further down the street. Then to some mice. And again the day after to another pair of rats. Gradually all the rats and mice became convinced that the cat had really changed its ways and was trying to be a genuine holy cat. They got used to him walking by reading, taking no notice of them.

Finally the rats and mice lost all their terror of the cat. One day two rats saw him coming down the street, and because they had no fear of him any more, carried on nibbling at a bit of bread that someone had dropped. These two rats happened to be the two plump female rats that the holy cat, before he had been on his pilgrimage, especially used to fancy. In the days before he became saintly, he'd been fond of crouching down with his head on his paws gazing at their rat holes in the wall, occasionally twitching the sides of his mouth in sheer longing. But the plump female rats had been too wily, and the cat had never got near either of them.

On this particular morning, though, they carried on quietly nibbling. They knew that since his pilgrimage the cat no longer hunted, but lived on dates and plain bread and devoted his life to holiness and sacred things.

And so the cat came walking by, muttering words from his Holy Book. If you'd been looking hard at him you'd have seen a tiny tremble of mouth and a twitch of whisker just before he—aaarrgh!—pounced! He grabbed them both in his mouth and trotted off around the corner.

A very unholy act for a holy cat!

The rats and mice forgot something rats and mice should always remember—that a cat that has been on a pilgrimage and reads holy books is still a cat.

Session Design for "A Holy Cat"

Materials

- a book

Story Drama Activities

1. MOTIVATE children by doing one or more of the following:

a. Discuss the concept of trust. Ask players which people they trust. Discuss what makes us trust and prevents us from trusting others.

b. Discuss the adage "Playing cat and mouse," and how its origin is rooted in the behavior of cats around mice.

c. If allowed, discuss how religious conversion may change people's behavior (or, how one might change from being evil to being good).

2. PRESENT the story: Since the story is played holistically, save the retelling of "A Holy Cat" for the end of the session.

3. DRAMATIZE the story:

a. Discuss how "word-of-mouth" makes news spread. The leader announces she will take on the role of a cat. Ask for two volunteers to play mice. The two volunteers are taken to a corner of the room. The mice are asked to position and locate themselves as if they are eavesdropping on the cat's conversation. As quietly and secretly as possible, the leader tells an imaginary friend she is going to the Holy City on a pilgrimage and will be back soon. Elaborate what is mentioned in the story, such as the length of time you may be gone and why you are going. The leader then announces she is out of role and addresses the entire class: "These two mice have heard some news and they are now going to spread it to the mouse and rat communities. Each of you tell one person in the class what you heard the cat say, and once someone else knows what's going on, tell someone else. You might even discuss with some of your friends what you think this might mean. Go spread the news to others about what you heard the cat tell her friend." Observe as children spread the news among each other. If needed, participate as a fellow mouse among the class and share, "I heard a rat say the cat was going to . . . ."

b. Gather players in a circle seated on the floor and announce you are going into role as a mouse. "Fellow mice and rats, I have heard some disturbing news and ridiculous stories about a certain cat who has been terrorizing us. Rumors and gossip are flying all over and driving us into needless worry. Let's try to piece this story together to make some sense of it and get to the truth. Now, what's going on? What have you heard?" Players are asked to volunteer their answers. If some news unrelated to the story is created spontaneously by children, allow them to share their tales but question their rumors with skepticism: "I heard that story too, but one of the mice who was actually there told me it didn't happen that way" or "Well, that sounds like something the cat wouldn't do. Are you sure that's what you heard?" As needed, help clarify for children what it means to go on a pilgrimage to the Holy City.

c. Announce that everyone is now out of role as mice. Share what was actually said in role as the cat during the first part of the playing and compare it to the stories the class developed. Discuss why the news may have been distorted or embellished. Also discuss why it would be so unusual for a cat to go on a pilgrimage.

d. The leader announces she will be going back into role as the cat and will be exhibiting unusual behaviors. Solicit two or three volunteers from the class who, as mice, will be "brave enough" to go to the cat and ask where she has been and if she has any news to tell them. Proceed to a corner of the room, announce that you are in role and the mice should approach the cat. The leader reads a book and mutters to herself, looking absorbed in her thoughts. Assist the volunteers, as needed, to initiate dialogue. Share with the mice that you have been to the Holy City and have realized it is wrong to hunt and eat mice and rats. State that you now eat only bread, and the rodents no longer have to worry about being killed. Encourage the mice to spread the news to others and bid them good day. Observe the news being spread among the class.

e. The leader announces she is out of role as the cat and brings the class together. Announce that you are stepping into role as a mouse: "Fellow rodents, I have heard another rumor about the cat and I can't believe my ears. Is it true that she's given up eating mice and rats forever?" Dialogue with children and solicit what they've heard. Discuss whether such a story—and the cat—can be trusted. Develop tales of how the cat has killed several friends in the past. Plant suspicion in the community.

f. Drop out of role and discuss the issues of suspicion and trust at stake for the rodents. Ask players to describe how the rodents would behave if they saw the cat approaching them: "If your life was as stake, how much trust would you show toward the cat?" Announce you will be going into role as the cat and walking through the alleyways of the community. Ask players to demonstrate suspicion and mistrust through their faces and bodies as the cat passes by them: "You'll need to be as quiet as possible. Screaming or running away would draw too much attention. Silence and stillness might be a better way to protect yourself." Walk through the classroom with the book. Stare at players intently as you walk by, nodding hello and occasionally smiling. Converse with a few mice, reinforcing that they needn't be afraid because you've changed your ways.

g. Announce that all are out of role and ask, "What thoughts were going through your mind as the cat walked by you?" Discuss and elaborate on the concept of trust and other issues children generate. Then discuss how the cat's nonviolent behavior might change the rodent's thoughts, beliefs, and attitudes: "What did the mice think and believe about the cat before he left for the Holy Land?" "If you saw after a long time that the cat was no longer a threat, what would you begin to believe? What new kinds of thoughts, attitudes, or feelings would the rodents have toward the cat?" Allow players to share expected answers but also solicit more in-depth responses ("You might trust the cat, but you'll always remember what he used to do in the past.").

h. Drop into role again as the cat and walk through the alleyways, asking children to demonstrate through their faces and bodies what they now think and believe about the cat. Converse with the mice, as needed. Announce to the rodent community you would like to invite them to your home for a dinner of bread, dates, and milk. Drop out of role and ask the rodents who will trust the cat and accept his invitation. If a discussion or debate among the rodent community emerges, facilitate the weighing of pros and cons. Those who accept are brought into a circle in one area of the room. Those who do not accept are separated to another part of the room. Join the circle that accepted the invitation and retell "A Holy Cat." (Note: The character genders in the climax—female rats eaten by a male cat—could be changed in the retelling for purposes of avoiding stereotypes.) Announce that those who joined the cat for dinner were the dinner, and those who chose not to join were spared.

4. ASSESS the dramatization:

a. Ask players to explain their motivations for accepting or refusing the cat's invitation to dinner. Solicit their personal responses upon learning the outcome of the story drama.

b. Discuss the themes in the story and life lessons about trust.

c. Discuss why the cat was not able to change his behavior. Ask players what he needed to do if he were to truly keep to his new way of life.

Social Studies Follow-Up

1. Locate North Africa and Mecca on a globe or map.

2. Discuss the Islamic religion and the practice of pilgrimage to Mecca. In what countries is the religion generally practiced by the majority or a small minority of the people? In what countries are followers of this religion in conflict with others?

3. Discuss how thoughts, beliefs, and attitudes work when we encounter people we trust or mistrust and people different from ourselves or our community.

Language Arts/Literature Follow-Up

1. Locate and read stories from other cultures that feature cats as prominent characters. Dramatize these stories if they lend themselves to improvisation.

2. Read selections from Aesop's fables and compare them with "A Holy Cat." How is "A Holy Cat" similar in structure to a fable?

3. Discuss how the religion of a culture influences its literature.

4. Compare "A Holy Cat" with "The Ten Farmers" in Chapter Five. How are the cultures' religions or religious themes woven into the stories?

"LITTLE EIGHT JOHN"

This story from the Aswell et al. collection has been slightly revised in word choice but not in the original sentence structure or grammar. This African American cautionary tale is deliciously humorous and poses challenges to the players on establishing environments—time and place—and depicting specific consequences through action.

The story can be dramatized in ensemble or small groups, depending on the age of the children and amount of drama experience they have had. Ensemble play (with the leader as Little Eight John's mother) may work best for grades 2–3, and small groups (with the leader as facilitator) for those in grade 4 with some previous drama experience.

Once and long ago there was a little black child name of Eight John. He was a nice lookin little boy but he didn't act like he look. He a mean little boy and he wouldn't mind a word the grown folks told him. No, not a livin word. So if his lovin mama told him not to do a thing, he go straight and do it. Yes, spite of all the world.

"Don't step on no toad-frogs," his lovin mama told him, "or you bring the bad luck on your family. Yes you will."

Little Eight John he say, "No'm, I won't step on no toad-frogs. No ma'am!"

But just as sure as anything, soon as he got out of sight of his lovin mama, that Little Eight John find him a toad-frog and squish it. Sometime he squish a heap of toad-frogs.

And the cow wouldn't give no milk but bloody milk and the baby would have the bad ol colic.

But Little Eight John he just duck his head and laugh.

"Don't set in no chair backwards," his lovin mama told Eight John. "It brings the weary troubles to your family."

And so Little Eight John he set backwards in every chair.

Then his lovin mama's cornbread burn and the milk wouldn't churn.

Little ol Eight John just laugh and laugh and laugh cause he know why it was.

"Don't climb no trees on Sunday," his lovin mama told him, "or it'll be bad luck."

So that Little Eight John, that bad little boy, he sneak up trees on Sunday.

Then his papa's taters wouldn't grow and the mule wouldn't go.

Little Eight John he know how come.

"Don't count your teeth," his lovin mama she tell Little Eight John, "or there come a bad sickness in your family."

But that Little Eight John he go right ahead and count his teeth. He count his uppers and he count his lowers. He count em on weekdays and Sundays.

Then his mama she whoop and the baby got the croup. All on account of that Little Eight John, that badness of a little ol boy.

"Don't sleep with your head at the foot of the bed or your family get the weary money blues," his lovin mama told him.

So he do it and do it sure, that cross-goin little ol Eight John boy.

And the family it went broke with no money in the poke. Little Eight John he just giggle.

"Don't have no Sunday moans, for fear Ol Raw Head Bloody Bones," his lovin mama told him.

So he had the Sunday moans and he had the Sunday groans, and he moan and he groan and he moan.

And Ol Raw Head Bloody Bones he come after that little bad boy and change him to a little ol grease spot on the kitchen table and his lovin mama wash it off the next mornin.

And that was the end of Little Eight John.

And that's what always happens to never-mindin little boys.

Session Design for "Little Eight John"

Story Drama Activities

1. MOTIVATE children by doing one or more of the following:

a. Discuss with children the consequences for not following the rules set by parents. Discuss why we sometimes do what we are told not to do.

b. Discuss superstitions and how they came to be. For example, ask why some consider it bad luck to walk under a ladder. What might the consequences be?

c. Play a game of Opposites. The leader calls out words or phrases and children are to do exactly the opposite. Things that might be called out are: "sit," "say 'yes'," "stand still," "look at me," "don't touch your nose." Conclude the game with "stand up" and tell children the game is completed.

2. PRESENT the story: Leaders are encouraged to retell the story in a straightforward manner without any attempt at dialect. If leaders will be reading the story as written directly from the book, share that the language is based on what was considered by the writer during the middle of the century as rural folk dialect.

3. DRAMATIZE the story: (The session is designed for small-group work. Leaders can modify the playing for ensemble if children have not had sufficient small-group experiences in drama.)

  a. Discuss how time and place (i.e., "setting") can be established through dramatic action and/or dialogue. Ask how a farm setting might be depicted through physical action. Have players dramatize their suggestions nonverbally in ensemble. Next, discuss and dramatize how evening can be depicted through nonverbal and verbal methods. A final task for older children is to ask how dramatic action can be used to suggest that the day is Sunday, aside from stating "Today is Sunday." Discuss ideas with children and dramatize them through ensemble play, or through a demonstration by a solo or pair playing shared with the class.

  b. Have all players find their own space in the room. In ensemble, ask players to find solutions for dramatizing the following consequences of Little Eight John's behavior:
    1. milking a cow and discovering the milk is bad

    2. taking care of (or portraying) a baby sick from colic

    3. showing that your cornbread is burnt

    4. churning milk that will not turn to butter

    5. discovering potatoes that won't grow

    6. trying to get a mule to move

    7. having the whooping cough

    8. taking care of (or portraying) a baby sick from croup

    9. losing your money; having no money

    Observe and assess the players' work. As needed, help children find solutions to portray the actions.

  c. Divide players into small groups of three or four. Although a small group composed of both boys and girls may assist with casting according to gender, same-gender groups are also appropriate. It is not essential that Mama be played only by girls, or that Little Eight John be played only by boys. Assign each group a unit of action in the story to dramatize according to the order they occur in the story. Members of each group distribute the roles among themselves.

1. UNIT ONE: After Mama warns Little Eight John not to step on toad-frogs, he does it anyway. The cow gives bad milk and the baby gets colic.

2. UNIT TWO: After Mama warns Little Eight John not to sit backward in a chair, he does it anyway. The cornbread burns and the butter will not churn.

3. UNIT THREE: After Mama warns Little Eight John not to climb trees on Sunday, he does it anyway. His father's potatoes do not grow and the mule will not move.

4. UNIT FOUR: After Mama warns Little Eight John not to count his teeth, he does it anyway. His mother gets the whooping cough and the baby gets the croup.

5. UNIT FIVE: After Mama warns Little Eight John not to sleep with his head at the foot of the bed, he does it anyway. The family loses their money.

Allow players ten to fifteen minutes to develop their scenes through pantomime and verbal improvisation. Facilitate the presentation of the scenes in the order they occur in the story. Assess the effectiveness of each group in dramatizing the required action.

d. Discuss how the final unit of the story might be dramatized. Ask players to share ideas for how the character Ol Raw Head Bloody Bones might appear and be created (ensemble, small groups, etc.). Encourage children to develop a vocal characterization as well, but advise them that a noise does not have to be loud to be scary. Facilitate the enactment of children's ideas.

e. Discuss how Little Eight John's transformation from a boy to a grease spot can be portrayed. The following is suggested as one way of dramatizing the final unit, but if children develop another idea use theirs instead. Divide players into pairs, one portraying Little Eight John and the other portraying Ol Raw Head Bloody Bones. Discuss how children portraying the creature can approach their partners, transform them into grease without any physical contact, then leave. Once the ideas have been discussed, dramatize the unit: The leader as Mama warns Little Eight John not to have the "Sunday moans." Children portraying the boy do the opposite; their partners as the creature approach Little Eight John and transform him into a grease spot. The leader as Mama sees the "grease" and wipes it with an imaginary rag. Have players reverse roles and replay the unit.

4. ASSESS the dramatization:

a. Discuss the ability of children to dramatize the settings (environments) and actions depicted in the story.

b. Assess the ability of players to work independently in small groups. Discuss what dynamics contributed to effective group work.

c. Discuss why Little Eight John did the opposite of what he was told. What reasons or motivations did he have for being contrary?

Social Studies Follow-Up

1. List the elements in this story that depict the setting. What components of rural farm life are mentioned in the tale?

2. Discuss why this story exists. What purpose might it have served when it was created?

3. Compare the characters of Ol Raw Head Bloody Bones and Auntie Tiger (see Chapter Five) as figures used to frighten or warn children. Discuss other cultures that have such characters in their folk literature and discuss why people create these characters.

Language Arts/Literature Follow-Up

1. This version of "Little Eight John" was written to capture a sense of rural folk dialect. How would the story change if it were rewritten in Standard English with correct grammar and spelling? What would be gained? What would be lost?

2. Compare this story to "Fatima and the Snake" in this chapter. How are Fatima and Little Eight John's characters and problems similar? different?

3. Discuss the use of Black English by some African Americans today. Examine why it exists and why it is used in conversation. Compare Black English to "Spanglish" spoken by some Hispanics. What do the two languages have in common?

4. Read selected stories from Virginia Hamilton's *The People Could Fly* (New York: Alfred A. Knopf, 1985). Discuss what choices Ms. Hamilton makes with language to create a unique writing style for

retelling the folktales. Dramatize those stories that lend themselves to improvisation.

"PEOPLE WHO COULD FLY"

Grades 5–6 can explore dramatizing Lester's dynamic retelling of this African American folktale. Particular challenges to the group are maintaining commitment, a serious tone during the dramatization, and the enactment of people flying.

    If the leader reads this story as written, a preparatory discussion about the writer's use of the term "nigger" is essential. Teachers are encouraged to use their own judgment when explaining the term's historical context and the writer's choice of the term in this story.

It happened long, long ago, when black people were taken from their homes in Africa and forced to come here to work as slaves. They were put onto ships, and many died during the long voyage across the Atlantic Ocean. Those that survived stepped off the boats into a land they had never seen, a land they never knew existed, and they were put into the fields to work.

    Many refused, and they were killed. Others would work, but when the white man's whip lashed their backs to make them work harder, they would turn and fight. And some of them killed the white men with the whips. Others were killed by the white men. Some would run away and try to go back home, back to Africa where there were no white people, where they worked their own land for the good of each other, not for the good of white men. Some of those who tried to go back to Africa would walk until they came to the ocean, and then they would walk into the water, and no one knows if they did walk to Africa through the water or if they drowned. It didn't matter. At least they were no longer slaves.

    Now when the white man forced Africans onto the slave-ships, he did not know, nor did he care, if he took the village musicians, artists, or witch doctors. As long as they were black and looked strong, he wanted them—men, women, and children. Thus, he did not know that sometimes there would be a witch doctor among those he had captured. If he had known, and had also known that the witch doctor was the medium of the gods, he would have thought twice. But he did not care. These black men and black women were not people to him. He looked at them and counted each one as so much money for his pocket.

It was to a plantation in South Carolina that one boatload of Africans was brought. Among them was the son of a witch doctor who had not completed by many months studying the secrets of the gods from his father. This young man carried with him the secrets and powers of the generations of Africa.

One day, one hot day when the sun singed the very hair on the head, they were working in the fields. They had been in the fields since before the sun rose, and, as it made its journey to the highest part of the sky, the very air seemed to be on fire. A young woman, her body curved with the child that grew deep inside her, fainted.

Before her body struck the ground, the white man with the whip was riding toward her on his horse. He threw water in her face. "Get back to work, you lazy nigger! There ain't going to be no sitting down on the job as long as I'm here." He cracked the whip against her back and, screaming, she staggered to her feet.

All work had stopped as the Africans watched, saying nothing.

"If you niggers don't want a taste of the same, you'd better get to work!"

They lowered their heads and went back to work. The young witch doctor worked his way slowly toward the young mother-to-be, but before he could reach her, she collapsed again, and the white man with the whip was upon her, lashing her until her body was raised from the ground by the sheer violence of her sobs. The young witch doctor worked his way to her side and whispered something in her ear. She, in turn, whispered to the person beside her. He told the next person, and on around the field it went. They did it so quickly and quietly that the white man with the whip noticed nothing.

A few moments later, someone else in the field fainted, and, as the white man with the whip rode toward him, the young witch doctor shouted, "Now!" He uttered a strange word, and the person who had fainted rose from the ground, and moving his arms like wings, he flew into the sky and out of sight.

The man with the whip looked around at the Africans, but they only stared into the distance, tiny smiles softening their lips. "Who did that? Who was that who yelled out?" No one said anything. "Well, just let me get my hands on him."

Not too many minutes had passed before the young woman fainted once again. The man was almost upon her when the young witch doctor shouted, "Now!" and uttered a strange word. She, too, rose from the ground and, waving her arms like wings, she flew into the distance and out of sight.

This time the man with the whip knew who was responsible, and as he pulled back his arm to lash the young witch doctor, the young man yelled, "Now! Now! Everyone!" He uttered the strange word, and all of the Africans dropped their hoes, stretched out their arms, and flew away, back to their home, back to Africa.

That was long ago, and no one now remembers what word it was that the young witch doctor knew that could make people fly. But who knows? Maybe one morning someone will awake with a strange word on his tongue and, uttering it, we will all stretch out our arms and take to the air, leaving these blood-drenched fields of our misery behind.

Session Design for "People Who Could Fly"

Story Drama Activities

1. MOTIVATE children by doing one or more of the following:
   a. Provide a brief overview of slave ownership in early United States history.

   b. Ask players about the connotations of people flying without the use of machines. What associations are made with the ability of people who can fly?

   c. Discuss what players need to do for an effective dramatization of a serious piece of literature.

2. PRESENT the story: Read aloud Julius Lester's version of the story, or retell the tale in your own way for the players.

3. DRAMATIZE the story:
   a. Discuss what it means to be defiant. Ask players how slaves might have felt before refusing to carry out an order from their owners. Ask what might be done physically and vocally to portray defiance of an order. The class reviews tasks slaves were forced to perform (both indoors and outdoors). Ask players to get into groups of two or three. Allow players within their own groups to select who will portray the owner(s) and who will portray the slave(s). Address the issue of "nontraditional" casting (see Chapter Two) and specify that one's own ethnicity does not have to be a factor in casting appropriately. Then ask players to select one of the tasks discussed earlier that the slave(s) will be ordered to perform. Once these decisions have been made, provide further directions for playing: "Your group will be presenting a fifteen-second scene. It can begin with the owners telling the slaves to do the tasks you've selected. The slaves will defy the orders, and that might generate a reaction from

the owners. The scene can end with the slaves still not carrying out the task. Fifteen seconds of dialogue and tension are all you need." Remind the group of guidelines for this scene: no physical contact (pushing, hitting, etc.) between characters; no harsh or inappropriate language (profanity, racist terms); and commitment and believability to the characters. Reinforce the idea that tension is not necessarily created by what is said, or through loud and angry voices, but by how it's said and shown. Allow players approximately five minutes to prepare, then facilitate the sharing of their presentations. Assess the players' ability to follow established guidelines and generate tension in their brief scenes.

b. Discuss what the specific consequences may have been for the actions portrayed in the scenes, based on the story's general description of outcome. Ask players what motivates and characterizes those who abuse control and those who defy that control. Ask what circumstances may have existed for the slaves in the field as depicted in Lester's story that kept them from defying orders before then. Focus on why no one rescued the pregnant slave the first time she was whipped. Discuss whatever emotional states may be raised through discussion, such as hopelessness, fear, or apathy, and how they relate to the slave characters.

c. Discuss what specific field crop is the setting for the story, and what tools or human activities would be needed for working on it. Ask players to line themselves in columns in the space, similar to the way a crop might be planted, and begin working on the crop. Sidecoach imagery that motivates players to depict the outdoor heat: "Working as believably as you can, without playing for laughs, and committing to the action as hard as you can, show through your actions that you're working on this crop and trying to stay cool on this hot, hot day. Try to show through your face the glaring sunlight, the sweat that drips into and burns your eyes; through your body show the physical labor you're undertaking. Through your silence there is much that is not said. Try to imagine what these people must have been thinking about as they were working hard on this day, and the feelings these circumstances generated within them. Using your body and face alone, try to re-create this scene from long ago." Observe the action and allow time for players to commit. If necessary, the leader can walk around the space and sidecoach in role to the players: "Get to work, if you know what's good for you. This ain't no time to be lazy; we got this whole field to take care of before sundown." If desired, the leader can prompt out of role, "Keep working. I'm going to tap some of you on the shoulder. Verbalize a phrase or sentence that represents what your character might be thinking or feeling at this time." Select a few or all players to respond. Ask players to relax. Discuss whether believability and commitment were evident in the work.

d. Ask players to negotiate and agree on the "strange word" spoken by the young witch doctor that gave others the power to fly. Next ask the group how whipping and getting whipped might be panto-mimed. If possible, develop a sound effect to accompany the gesture of whipping. (In one session the group agreed the whip would be cracked three times in a row as all vocalized a synchronized *sss* sound with each strike.) Then ask how the action of flying might be depicted in a dramatization of the next scene, given the limitations of space in the room. Discuss possible solutions to this problem and enact them with the whole group. Develop a method of bringing closure to the scene when all fly away at the end of the story (e.g., where players will stop, the final line of dialogue to end the scene).

e. Select volunteers or assign players to portray the pregnant slave, the young witch doctor, and the other man who faints. The leader may choose to play in role as the man with the whip, or assign a student to portray the character. Practice and run through the action of this unit in Lester's story before dramatizing it "from beginning to end with no stops." After the dramatization, assess the work. If player interest is still evident, recast the characters and replay the unit.

4. ASSESS the dramatization:

a. Discuss the players' ability to maintain a serious tone and commitment to the playing. Ask what made it difficult or easy to stay believable.

b. Explore the slaves' emotional reactions at various points throughout the story. Ask players if any of these same feelings may have been generated within themselves when they portrayed the characters.

c. Ask players what scenic elements or special effects would be needed if this story were to be dramatized on the stage or in electronic media. What technical challenges await the scenic artist, cinematographer, and visual effects designer?

d. Ask players to reflect on and identify personal situations in which we or others are "slaves" to authorities or controlling factors in our lives. What methods can be employed to counteract these authorities or controlling factors?

Social Studies Follow-Up

1. Examine on a globe or map the passages across the Atlantic Ocean from Africa to the United States that might have been used by slave ships in the eighteenth and nineteenth centuries.

2. Examine the historic events of civil unrest and interethnic relations in America during the late 1960s (the period Julius Lester wrote and first published this story). Discuss how that era may have influenced Lester's writing and tone of "People Who Could Fly," and why the story was also relevant to the late 1960s (and today).

3. Ask players to reflect on other historic or contemporary contexts of oppressed people. In what ways could the content or theme of the story be relevant to other countries or time periods?

4. Ask players to describe what motivates humans to action when they feel their personal rights are violated, or when they feel "enough is enough." What human qualities or material objects give a person power to control or make that person feel superior to others? How might that power and control be lessened, overthrown, or taken away by the controlled and powerless? Improvise original scenarios on these themes developed by the class.

Language Arts/Literature Follow-Up

1. Read other stories from Julius Lester's collection, *Black Folktales* (New York: Grove Weidenfeld, 1970). Dramatize such tales as "Why Men Have to Work."

2. Compare Julius Lester's version of "People Who Could Fly" with Virginia Hamilton's title story in *The People Could Fly* (New York: Alfred A. Knopf, 1985). In what ways are their versions of the stories similar and different?

3. Discuss flying as a symbol or metaphor. Ask students what emotions or meanings are evoked by the fantasy of humans with the ability to fly. Search for folktales from other cultures that include the flying motif. Compare the symbolic interpretation of flying from these folktales to the connotations of flying from "People Who Could Fly."

4. Discuss *sympathy* (feeling sorry for someone else) and *empathy* (feeling the same emotion as someone else). Examine passages in "People Who Could Fly" that may evoke sympathy and/or empathy from its readers. What choices does the writer make with description, dialogue, and action to generate sympathy and/or empathy?

References

Introduction

Arizona Department of Education. 1990a. *Arizona Essential Skills for Performing Arts K–12: Dramatic Arts.* Phoenix: Arizona Department of Education.

———. 1990b. *Literature Essential Skills.* Phoenix: Arizona Department of Education.

———. 1989a. *The Language Arts Essential Skills.* Phoenix: Arizona Department of Education.

———. 1989b. *Social Studies Essential Skills.* Phoenix: Arizona Department of Education.

ASU Center for Bilingual Education and Research. 1990. *El Portavoz,* November: 1–3.

Banks, James A. 1994. *Multiethnic Education.* 3d ed. Needham Heights, MA: Allyn and Bacon.

———. 1987. The Social Studies, Ethnic Diversity, and Social Change. *The Elementary School Journal* 87(5):531–43.

Banks, James A., and Cherry A. McGee Banks, eds. 1993. *Multicultural Education: Issues and Perspectives.* 2d ed. Needham Heights, MA: Allyn and Bacon.

Consortium of National Arts Education Associations. 1994. *National Standards for Arts Education.* Reston, VA: Music Educators National Conference.

Gray, Paul. 1993. Teach Your Children Well. *Time* 142(21):68–71.

Marvel, Bill, and Barbara Kessler. 1994. Timetable of Political Correctness. *The Arizona Republic* 8 May.

Chapter One

Ritch, Pamela. 1983. A Good Substitute for Recess in Winter: Some Elementary Classroom Teacher's Perceptions About Creative Drama: An Informal Report. *Children's Theatre Review* 32(4):3–8.

Chapter Two

(includes additional sources not cited in the text)

Allen, Judy, Earldene McNeill, and Velma Schmidt. 1992. *Cultural Awareness for Children.* Menlo Park, CA: Addison-Wesley.

Aoki, Elaine. 1992. "Turning the Page: Asian Pacific American Children's Literature." In *Teaching Multicultural Literature in Grades K–8,* edited by Violet J. Harris, 109–35. Norwood, MA: Christopher-Gordon.

Banks, James A. 1994. *Multiethnic Education.* 3d ed. Needham Heights, MA: Allyn and Bacon.

Banks, James A., and Cherry A. McGee Banks, eds. 1993. *Multicultural Education: Issues and Perspectives.* 2d ed. Needham Heights, MA: Allyn and Bacon.

Baruth, Leroy G., and M. Lee Manning. 1992. *Multicultural Education of Children and Adolescents.* Needham Heights, MA: Allyn and Bacon.

Bennett, Christine I. 1986. *Comprehensive Multicultural Education.* Needham Heights, MA: Allyn and Bacon.

Brown, Norman. 1994. Interview by author. Tape recording. Tempe, AZ. 14 January.

Buege, Carol. 1993. The Effect of Mainstreaming on Attitude and Self-Concept Using Creative Drama and Social Skills Training. *Youth Theatre Journal* 7(3):19–22.

Burstein, Nancy Davis, and Beverly Cabello. 1989. Preparing Teachers to Work with Culturally Diverse Students: A Teacher Education Model. *Journal of Teacher Education* 40(5):9–16.

Chan, Kenyon S. 1983. "Limited English Speaking, Handicapped, and Poor: Triple Threat in Childhood." In *Asian- and Pacific-American Perspectives in Bilingual Education: Comparative Research,* edited by Mae Chu-Chuang and Victor Rodriguez, 153–71. New York: Teachers College Press.

Chu-Chuang, Mae, and Victor Rodriguez, eds. 1983. *Asian- and Pacific-American Perspectives in Bilingual Education: Comparative Research.* New York: Teachers College Press.

Comer, James P., and Alvin F. Poussaint. 1992. *Raising Black Children.* New York: Penguin Books.

Doyle, Don. 1994. Interview by author. Tape recording. Mesa, AZ. 7 March.

Dunn, Judith Ann. 1977. The Effect of Creative Dramatics on the Oral Language Abilities and Self-Esteem of Blacks, Chicanos and Anglos in the Second and Fifth Grades. Ph.D. diss., University of Colorado.

Erdman, Harley. 1991. Conflicts of Interest: Bringing Drama to the Elementary Foreign Language Classroom. *Youth Theatre Journal* 5(3):12–14.

Finer, Neal Bentley. 1990. Interview by author. Tape recording. Tempe, AZ. 12 December.

Foreman, Kathleen. 1991. Native Teaching and Learning/Dramatic Teaching and Learning. *Youth Theatre Journal* 5(3):16–20.

Fraire, Mark J. 1994. Letter to author, 15 June.

Garcia, Anamarie. 1990. Interview by author. Tape recording. Scottsdale, AZ. 16 November.

Gay, Geneva. 1993. "Ethnic Minorities and Educational Equality." In *Multicultural Education: Issues and Perspectives*, 2d ed., edited by James A. Banks and Cherry A. McGee Banks, 171–94. Needham Heights, MA: Allyn and Bacon.

Gimmestad, Beverly J., and Edith De Chiara. 1982. Dramatic Plays: A Vehicle for Prejudice Reduction in the Elementary School. *The Journal for Educational Research* 76(1):45–49.

Gonzalez, Roseann Duenas. 1990. When Minority Becomes Majority: The Changing Face of English Classrooms. *English Journal* 79(1):16–23.

Gourgey, Annette F., Jason Bosseau, and Judith Delgado. 1985. The Impact of an Improvisational Dramatic Program on Student Attitudes and Achievement. *Children's Theatre Review* 34(3): 9–14.

Hale, Janice. 1983. "Black Children: Their Roots, Culture, and Learning Styles." In *Understanding the Multicultural Experience in Early Childhood Education*, edited by Olivia N. Saracho and Bernard Spodek, 17–34. Washington, D.C.: National Association for the Education of Young Children.

Haley, Gary Ann Lyons. 1978. Training Advantaged and Disadvantaged Black Kindergarteners in Socio-drama: Effects on Creativity and Free Recall Variables of Oral Language. Ph.D. diss., University of Georgia.

Hendrickson, Richard H., and Frances S. Gallegos. 1972. "Using Creative Dramatics to Improve the English Language Skills of Mexican-American Students: Final Report." ERIC, ED 077023.

Herman, Joan L., Pamela R. Aschbacher, and Lynn Winters. 1992. *A Practical Guide to Alternative Assessment*. Alexandria, VA: Association for Supervision and Curriculum Development.

Hill, Howard D. 1989. *Effective Strategies for Teaching Minority Students*. Bloomington, IN: National Educational Service.

Hudelson, Sarah. 1994. Interview by author. Tape recording. Tempe, AZ. 14 February.

Jordan, Cathie, Kathryn Hu-Pei Au, and Ann K. Joesting. 1983. "Patterns of Classroom Interaction with Pacific Islands Children: The Importance of Cultural Differences." In *Asian- and Pacific-American Perspectives in Bilingual Education: Comparative Research*, edited by Mae Chu-Chuang and Victor Rodriguez, 216–42. New York: Teachers College Press.

Kardash, Carol Anne M., and Lin Wright. 1987. Does Creative Drama Benefit Elementary School Students: A Meta-analysis. *Youth Theatre Journal* 1(3):11–18.

Kelin, Daniel A., II. 1994. Letter to author, 7 April.

Kelly, Mary J. 1994. Interview by author. Tape recording. Tempe, AZ. 21 January.

Kitano, Margie K. 1993. "Early Education for Asian-American Children." In *Understanding the Multicultural Experience in Early Childhood Education*, edited by Olivia N. Saracho and Bernard Spodek, 45–66. Washington, D.C.: National Association for the Education of Young Children.

Koester, Coleen. 1994. Interview by author. Tape recording. Tempe, AZ. 15 January.

Lê Pham Thúy-kim. 1994. Interview by author. Tape recording. Tempe, AZ. 25 February.

Lehon, John. 1994. Letter to author, 1 June.

Lynch, James. 1989. *Multicultural Education in a Global Society*. London: Falmer Press.

Martinez, Ruben, and Richard L. Dukes. 1987. Race, Gender and Self-esteem Among Youth. *Hispanic Journal of Behavioral Sciences* 9(4):427–43.

Matsumori, Hiroko. 1994. Interview by author. Tape recording. Tempe, AZ. 4 February.

Morris, Jeanne B. 1983. "Classroom Methods and Materials." In *Understanding the Multicultural Experience in Early Childhood Education*, edited by Olivia N. Saracho and Bernard Spodek, 77–90. Washington, D.C.: National Association for the Education of Young Children.

Niyekawa, Agnes M. 1983. "Biliteracy Acquisition and Its Sociocultural Effects." In *Asian- and Pacific-American Perspectives in Bilingual Education: Comparative Research*, edited by Mae Chu-Chuang and Victor Rodriguez, 97–119. New York: Teachers College Press.

Pesqueira, Virginia. 1994. Interview by author. Tape recording. Tempe, AZ. 21 February.

Quinn, Betsy. 1994. Letter to author, 1 May.

Randolph, Tracy Joy. 1994. Letter to author, 2 May.

Rosenberg, Helane. 1989. Transformations Described: How Twenty-Three Young People Think About and Experience Creative Drama. *Youth Theatre Journal* 4(1):21–27.

Saldaña, Johnny. 1994. "Because of the cultural differences . . ." Typescript.

———. 1991. Drama, Theatre and Hispanic Youth: Interviews with Selected Teachers and Artists. *Youth Theatre Journal* 5(4): 3–8.

Sanchez, Gilberto. 1994. This Hard Rock. *The Drama/Theatre Teacher* 6(3):12–17.

Saracho, Olivia N., and Bernard Spodek, eds. 1983. *Understanding the Multicultural Experience in Early Childhood Education.* Washington, D.C.: National Association for the Education of Young Children.

Shacker, Deborah L., Moira F. Juliebö, and Douglas Parker. 1993. Using Drama in the French Immersion Program. *Youth Theatre Journal* 8(1): 3–10.

Shade, Barbara J., and Clara A. New. 1993. "Cultural Influences on Learning: Teaching Implications." In *Multicultural Education: Issues and Perspectives*, 2d ed., edited by James A. Banks and Cherry A. McGee Banks, 317–31. Needham Heights, MA: Allyn and Bacon.

Spencer, D. David. 1994. Letter to author, 9 April.

Swierceski, Mary. 1993. Interviews by author. Tape recordings. Phoenix, AZ. 30 September, 15 October, 25 October.

Tafoya, Terry. 1983. "Coyote in the Classroom: The Use of American-Indian Oral Tradition with Young Children." In *Understanding the Multicultural Experience in Early Childhood Education*, edited by Olivia N. Saracho and Bernard Spodek, 35–44. Washington, D.C.: National Association for the Education of Young Children.

Treviño, Jesús. 1994. Interview by author. Tape recording. Tempe, AZ. 15 February.

Tsang, Chui-Lim. 1983. Code-Switching Strategies in Bilingual Instructional Settings. In *Asian- and Pacific-American American Perspectives in Bilingual Education: Comparative Research*, edited by Mae Chu-Chuang and Victor Rodriguez, 197–215. New York: Teachers College Press.

Tucker, JoAnne Klinem. 1971. The Use of Creative Dramatics as an Aid in Developing Reading Readiness with Kindergarten Children. Ph.D. diss., University of Wisconsin.

Vallejo, Carlos J. 1994. Interview by author. Tape recording. Tempe, AZ. 14 February.

Vitz, Kathie. 1984. The Effects of Creative Drama in English as a Second Language. *Children's Theatre Review* 33(2):23–26.

———. 1983. A Review of Empirical Research in Drama and Language. *Children's Theatre Review* 32(4):17–25.

Wagner, Betty Jane. 1988. Research Currents: Does Classroom Drama Affect the Arts of Language? *Language Arts* 65(1):46–55.

SELECTED BIBLIOGRAPHY

Drama with Children

Cattanach, Ann. 1992. *Drama for People with Special Needs*. London: A & C Black.

Chapman, Gerald. 1991. *Teaching Young Playwrights*. Portsmouth, NH: Heinemann.

Evans, Cheryl, and Lucy Smith. 1992. *Acting & Theatre*. London: Usborne.

Goodwillie, Barbara. 1986. *Breaking Through: Drama Strategies for the 10's to 15's*. Rowayton: New Plays.

Heinig, Ruth Beall. 1992. *Improvisation with Favorite Tales: Integrating Drama Into the Reading/Writing Classroom*. Portsmouth, NH: Heinemann.

———. 1988. *Creative Drama for the Classroom Teacher*. 3d ed. Englewood Cliffs, NJ: Prentice-Hall.

McCaslin, Nellie. 1990. *Creative Drama in the Classroom*. 5th ed. New York: Longman.

Morgan, Norah, and Juliana Saxton. 1987. *Teaching Drama*. Cheltenham: Stanley Thornes.

Neelands, Jonothan. 1984. *Making Sense of Drama*. London: Heinemann Educational Books.

Salisbury, Barbara T. 1986a. *Theatre Arts in the Elementary Classroom: Grade Four Through Grade Six*. New Orleans, LA: Anchorage Press.

———. 1986b. *Theatre Arts in the Elementary Classroom: Kindergarten Through Grade Three*. New Orleans, LA: Anchorage Press.

Stewig, John Warren, and Carol Buege. 1994. *Dramatizing Literature in Whole Language Classrooms*. 2d ed. New York: Teachers College Press.

Way, Brian. 1967. *Development Through Drama*. Atlantic Highlands: Humanities Press.

Storytelling

Baker, Augusta, and Ellin Green. 1987. *Storytelling: Art and Technique*, 2d ed. New York: R. R. Bowker Company.

Cooper, Pamela J., and Rives Collins. 1992. *Look What Happened to Frog: Storytelling in Education*. Scottsdale, AZ: Gorsuch Scaresburg Publishers.

Davis, Donald. 1993. *Telling Your Own Stories*. Little Rock, AK: August House Publishers.

Maguire, Jack. 1985. *Creative Storytelling: Choosing, Inventing and Sharing Tales for Children*. New York: McGraw-Hill.

Livo, Norma J., and Sandra A. Rietz. 1986. *Storytelling: Process and Practice*. Littleton, CO: Libraries Unlimited.

Pellowski, Anne. 1990. *The World of Storytelling*. Rev. ed. Bronx, NY: The H. W. Wilson Company.

MacDonald, Margaret Read. 1993. *The Storyteller's Start-Up Book: Finding, Learning, Performing, and Using Folktales*. Little Rock, AK: August House Publishers.

Sawyer, Ruth. 1947. *The Way of the Storyteller*. New York: Viking Press.

Shedlock, Marie L. 1951. *The Art of the Story-Teller*. 3d ed. New York: Dover Publications.

Multicultural and Multiethnic Education

(also see References for Chapter Two)

Allen, Judy, Earldene McNeill, and Velma Schmidt. 1992. *Cultural Awareness for Children*. Menlo Park, CA: Addison-Wesley.

Banks, James A. 1994. *Multiethnic Education*. 3d ed. Needham Heights, MA: Allyn and Bacon.

Banks, James A., and Cherry A. McGee Banks, eds. 1993. *Multicultural Education: Issues and Perspectives*. 2d ed. Needham Heights, MA: Allyn and Bacon.

———. 1995. *Handbook of Research on Multicultural Education*. New York: Macmillan.

Baruth, Leroy G., and M. Lee Manning. 1992. *Multicultural Education of Children and Adolescents*. Needham Heights, MA: Allyn and Bacon.

Harris, Violet J., ed. 1992. *Teaching Multicultural Literature in Grades K–8*. Norwood, MA: Christopher-Gordon.

Hill, Howard D. 1989. *Effective Strategies for Teaching Minority Students*. Bloomington, IN: National Education Service.

Kruse, Ginny Moore, Kathleen T. Horning, Merri V. Lindgren, and Katherine Odahowski. 1991. *Multicultural Literature for Children and Young Adults.* 3d ed. Madison: University of Wisconsin-Madison and the Wisconsin Department of Public Instruction.

Price, Clement Alexander. 1994. *Many Voices, Many Opportunities: Cultural Pluralism & American Arts Policy.* New York: American Council for the Arts.

Ramirez, Gonzalo, Jr., and Jan Lee Ramirez. 1994. *Multiethnic Children's Literature.* Albany: Delmar Publishers.

Saracho, Olivia N., and Bernard Spodek, eds. 1983. *Understanding the Multicultural Experience in Early Childhood Education.* Washington, D.C.: National Association for the Education of Young Children.

Saravia-Shore, Marietta, and Steven F. Arvizu, eds. 1992. *Cross-Cultural Literacy: Ethnographies of Communication in Multiethnic Classrooms.* New York: Garland.

Organizations

American Alliance for Theatre & Education
Department of Theatre
Arizona State University
Box 873411
Tempe, AZ 85287-3411
(602) 965-6064

National Storytelling Association
P. O. Box 309
Jonesborough, TN 37659
(800) 525-4514

National Association for Multicultural Education
c/o Donna M. Gollnick
2101A North Rolfe Street
Arlington, VA 22209-1007
(202) 416-6157

Saldaña, from a dance by choreographer Nikki Hu, who learned the story from Vietnamese children in Boston.

"Auntie Tiger" is collected from the oral tradition of Taiwanese stories, and adapted and retold by John Huang and Johnny Saldaña. From the handout prepared for the 1992 Arizona State University Summer Dance and Drama Institute.

"Taro and the Magic Fish" is collected from the oral tradition and retold by Johnny Saldaña.

"The Ten Farmers" from *Chinese Fairy Tales*. Copyright © 1946 and 1961 by The Peter Pauper Press, Inc. Reprinted by permission.

"Fatima and the Snake" from "Crocker at Risk Lessons," submitted by John Lehon. Collected from the oral tradition and retold by John Lehon and Johnny Saldaña.

"Anansi and the Sticky Man" is retold by Johnny Saldaña.

"A Holy Cat" from *African Stories* retold by Robert Hull. Copyright © 1992 by Wayland (Publishers) Ltd. Reprinted by permission of the publisher.

"Little Eight John" from *God Bless the Devil! Liars' Bench Tales* by James R. Aswell, Julia Willhoit, Jennette Edwards, E. E. Miller, and Lena Lipscomb. Copyright © 1940 by the University of North Carolina Press. Reprinted by permission.

"People Who Could Fly" from *Black Folktales* by Julius Lester (Grove Weidenfeld, 1970). Copyright © 1969 by Julius Lester. Reprinted by permission of the author.